THE PICTURE HISTORY

of

GREAT INVENTORS

Gillian Clements

To the inventors herein.
And to Geraldine and Emily Carter, Alison Effeny, and Peter Turvey,
with thanks for their help.

'I see you're admiring my little box,' the knight said in a friendly tone.
'It's my own invention – to keep clothes and sandwiches in.
You see I carry it upside-down, so that the rain can't get in.'

Alice's Adventures in Wonderland LEWIS CARROLL

The Picture History of Great Inventors
Text and illustrations copyright © 1993, 2000 Gillian Clements

Revised paperback edition published in Great Britain in 2000 by Frances Lincoln Limited,
4 Torriano Mews, Torriano Avenue, London NW5 2RZ.

First published in hardback in 1993 by Studio Editions Ltd, Princess House,
50 Eastcastle Street, London W1N 7AP, England.

British Library Cataloguing in Publication Data available on request

ISBN 0-7112-1605-3

Printed in Singapore

3 5 7 9 8 6 4 2

GILLIAN CLEMENTS was born in Sussex. Her childhood was spent
mainly on a farm where she remembers her father inventing things, like the
electric hurdle to stop foxes harming their
2,000 chickens. After reading Geography at Newcastle University,
she took a four-year degree course in Illustration at Brighton Polytechnic.
Since graduating Gillian has written and illustrated many popular children's
books for Macmillan, A & C Black and Scholastic. Her most recent titles
include, *Calligraphy Frenzy* (Scholastic), *Into the Underworld* (Walker).

THE PICTURE HISTORY
of
GREAT INVENTORS

Gillian Clements

FRANCES LINCOLN

CONTENTS

TO ALL INVENTORS OF THE FUTURE

If you enjoy this book then you might like to visit The Big Idea; the world's first 'inventor centre' and a permanent millennium exhibition. All of Gillian Clements's illustrations can be seen in this unique project which has been sponsored by the Nobel Exhibition Trust. Come and try out your ideas in its inventors' workshop, equipped with specially designed kits, tools and a testing bay, and experience the thrills of the History of Explosions theatre!

The exhibition is located on the Ardeer peninsula, on the West Coast of Scotland, and can be accessed from Irvine Harbourside via the Bridge of Scottish Invention. If you would like to learn more about The Big Idea, you can visit their website on www.bigidea.org.uk or contact them directly by phone on 01294 46-1999. Information and teachers' packs are available on request.

INTRODUCTION

One hundred years ago, or so, Henry Ford was building his first motor car, the Lumiéres were experimenting with moving pictures, and Marconi was finding a way to send messages by radio telegraph. Around seventy years later – within a life's span – the motor car had transformed into a moonbuggy, astronauts had spoken from Space by satellite radio-link, and moving pictures were showing images of men on the Moon!

Seeing is believing. I don't think that either Henry Ford, the Lumiére brothers, or Marconi could have imagined this future, let alone believed that any of these things might really happen. Yet they have, and the pace of change grows ever faster and faster. Can you imagine where our new technologies and inventions will take us and how they will change our lives? It's exciting and a bit frightening too.

All the inventors in this book have something in common I think – the challenge of solving problems, of finding new or better ways of doing things, of changing the future. It was fun for me to learn about their struggles and achievements. I hope you share my enjoyment.

Gillian Clements

THE EARLIEST INVENTIONS

The earliest civilisations arose along the great river valleys:
in China, Mesopotamia, Egypt, Greece and Rome.

GREECE

C.1650 BC	Sword
C.640 BC	Rooftiles
C.500 BC	Catapult
C.400 BC	Archytas of Taventum's Pulley
C.236 BC	Archimedes' Screw
C.150 BC	Astrolabe
AD C.100	Ptolemy's Earth-Centred Universe

ROME

C.350 BC	Roads
C.200 BC	Arched Bridges
C.150 BC	Screwpress
C.100 BC	Concrete
C.100 BC	Central Heating, Baths
C.50 BC	Groin Vault
C.20 BC	Aqueduct
C.10 BC	Crane
C. AD 100	Sandglass Timer
C. AD 79	Drawing Compass
C.100	Pantheon Dome

I, PTOLEMY, SAID THE EARTH WAS AT THE CENTRE OF THE UNIVERSE.

WHEE! WHEELS!

I'M CTESIBIUS

I'M IMHOTEP, A PYRAMID BUILDER

MMM, LOVELY BREAD

WHAT'S THE TIME?

River Euphrates

River Tigris

Jericho

Alexandria

Giza

Saqqara

Hero

EGYPT

C.5000–4000 BC	Copper Smelting
C.4500 BC	Grain Balance
C.3000 BC	Sailing Ship
3000–2800 BC	Pyramids at Giza and Saqqara
C.2000 BC	Shadow Clock
C.2000 BC	Bread Oven
C.1400 BC	Water Clock
C.1375 BC	Gondola
C.300–230 BC	Ctesibius' Inventions – Waterclock with Rack and Pinion Gear, Valves, Springs, Water Pump
C.285 BC	Pharos Lighthouse
C.190 BC	Parchment
C. AD 100	Hero's Turbine

MESOPOTAMIA

C.6000 BC	Bricks at Jericho
C.3500 BC	Kilns for Bricks
C.3500 BC	Plough
C.3500 BC	Potter's Wheel
C.3500 BC	Wheel
C.3000 BC	Arch at Ur
C.3000 BC	Abacus
C.1500 BC	Seed Drill
C. 700 BC	Tunnel Vault

NO-ONE KNOWS THE NAMES OF THE EARLIEST INVENTORS BUT MANY EGYPTIAN AND GREEK

Over 500,000 years ago fire is used for warmth.

40,000 years ago people reach Australia.

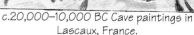

25,000 years ago, a bone shelter.

c.20,000–10,000 BC Cave paintings in Lascaux, France.

From c.8600 BC Farming develops along the great river valleys.

7000 BC The first looms.

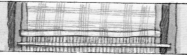

c.5000 BC Metal smelting of copper ores in Egypt.

5000 BC An early form of irrigation – the shaduf.

4000–3000 BC Potter's wheel in Sumeria.

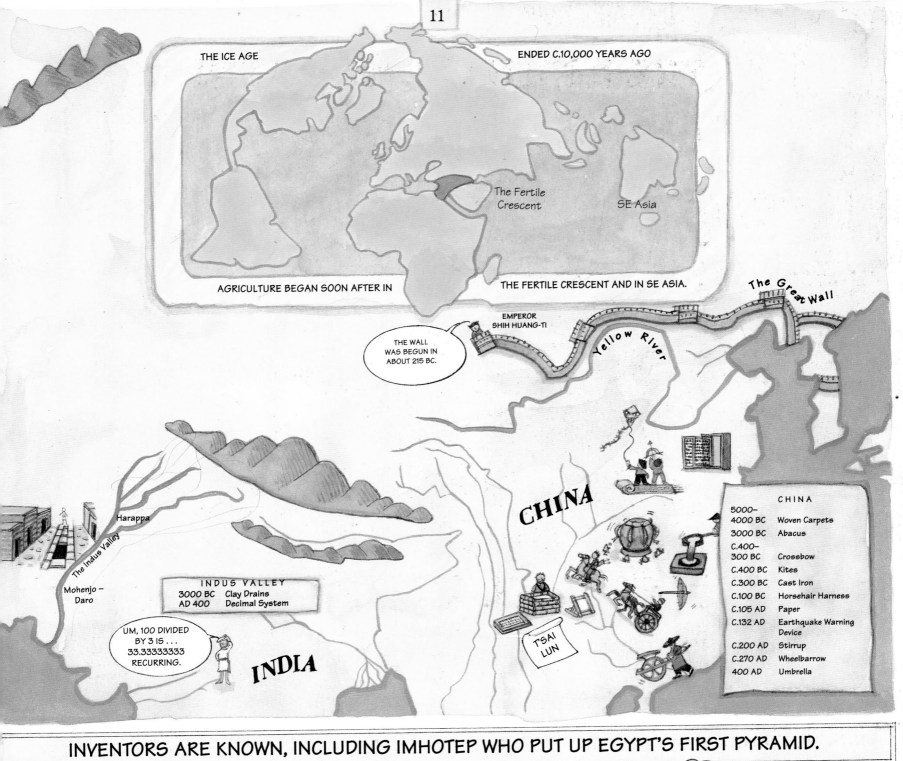

THE ICE AGE ENDED C.10,000 YEARS AGO

The Fertile Crescent

SE Asia

AGRICULTURE BEGAN SOON AFTER IN THE FERTILE CRESCENT AND IN SE ASIA.

The Great Wall

EMPEROR SHIH HUANG-TI

THE WALL WAS BEGUN IN ABOUT 215 BC.

Yellow River

CHINA

Harappa

The Indus Valley

Mohenjo – Daro

INDUS VALLEY

3000 BC	Clay Drains
AD 400	Decimal System

UM, 100 DIVIDED BY 3 IS . . . 33.33333333 RECURRING.

INDIA

TSAI LUN

CHINA	
5000–4000 BC	Woven Carpets
3000 BC	Abacus
C.400–300 BC	Crossbow
C.400 BC	Kites
C.300 BC	Cast Iron
C.100 BC	Horsehair Harness
C.105 AD	Paper
C.132 AD	Earthquake Warning Device
C.200 AD	Stirrup
C.270 AD	Wheelbarrow
400 AD	Umbrella

INVENTORS ARE KNOWN, INCLUDING IMHOTEP WHO PUT UP EGYPT'S FIRST PYRAMID.

From c.3500 BC

The development of writing: Sumer 3500 BC   Egypt c.3000 BC

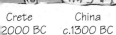

Crete 2000 BC   China c.1300 BC   Maya 250 AD   Phoenicia c.1000 BC

2700 BC – 2500 BC Great pyramids like those at Giza and Saqqara, are built in Egypt.

c.3500 BC The first wheeled vehicles.

3000 – 2000 BC Early examples of plumbing (Indus Valley and Crete).

800 – 700 BC Horseshoes are used in Europe.

287 B.C. ARCHIMEDES 212 B.C.

The brilliant Greek scientist, Archimedes, was born in Syracuse in Sicily. His best known invention was an improved machine for raising water, the 'Archimedes Screw'. He is also famous for his work on floating bodies, or buoyancy, the 'Archimedes Principle'.

Archimedes' many mechanical inventions and war machines made him popular in his day. His 'Archimedes Screw', for example, could be used for taking up water from ditches or for emptying flooded ships. He also explained how levers worked and how geometry could be used to measure circles.

Archimedes' war machines held off Roman attacks for three years, but in 212BC Syracuse was captured, and Archimedes was killed by a Roman soldier.

c. 250 BC Parchment – the skin of certain animals dried and shaved – is used to write on. Sheep skin is often used to make the parchment.

c. 230 BC Oil lamps begin to be used at this time in Greece about 18,000 years after their first use in China.

Archimedes' Principle: When a body is wholly or partially immersed in a fluid it appears to lose weight: i.e. it experiences an upward force equal to the weight of the fluid it displaces.

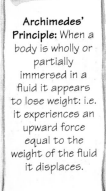

I'M BUOYED UP!

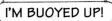

c. 224 BC Ctesibius of Alexandria invents the plunger pump.

c. 285 BC The Pharos lighthouse in Alexandria is finished.

HELP!

THE ARCHIMEDES SCREW

EUREKA!

THE WEIGHT OF THE WATER DISPLACED BY THE CROWN EQUALLED THE WEIGHT OF THE CROWN.

c. 215 BC The 2250 km long Great Wall of China is built to keep out barbarian invaders.

275 BC The Colossus of Rhodes is completed.

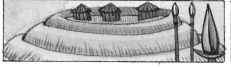

c. 250 BC Iron Age 'La Tène' people invade Britain.

c. 276–194 BC Eratosthenes makes a calculation of the Earth's circumference.

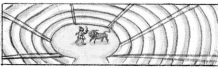

264 BC Gladiators take part in the first public contests in Rome.

HERO OF ALEXANDRIA
1st century AD

Hero's turbine

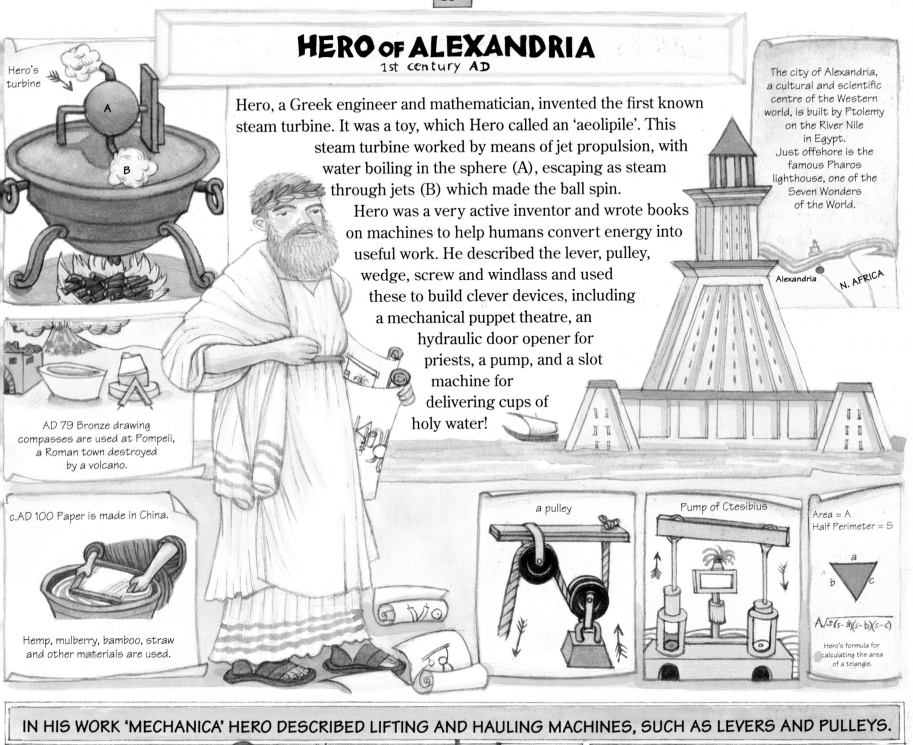

Hero, a Greek engineer and mathematician, invented the first known steam turbine. It was a toy, which Hero called an 'aeolipile'. This steam turbine worked by means of jet propulsion, with water boiling in the sphere (A), escaping as steam through jets (B) which made the ball spin.

Hero was a very active inventor and wrote books on machines to help humans convert energy into useful work. He described the lever, pulley, wedge, screw and windlass and used these to build clever devices, including a mechanical puppet theatre, an hydraulic door opener for priests, a pump, and a slot machine for delivering cups of holy water!

The city of Alexandria, a cultural and scientific centre of the Western world, is built by Ptolemy on the River Nile in Egypt. Just offshore is the famous Pharos lighthouse, one of the Seven Wonders of the World.

Alexandria   N. AFRICA

AD 79 Bronze drawing compasses are used at Pompeii, a Roman town destroyed by a volcano.

c.AD 100 Paper is made in China.

Hemp, mulberry, bamboo, straw and other materials are used.

a pulley

Pump of Ctesibius

Area = A
Half Perimeter = S

$$A\sqrt{s(s-a)(s-b)(s-c)}$$

Hero's formula for calculating the area of a triangle.

IN HIS WORK 'MECHANICA' HERO DESCRIBED LIFTING AND HAULING MACHINES, SUCH AS LEVERS AND PULLEYS.

c.AD 30 The crucifixion of Christ.

AFRICA

INDIA

AD 98–117 The Roman Empire under Emperor Trajan is at its largest extent.

AD 58 Buddhism is introduced into China from India.

AD 40 Greek sailors begin a new spice trade when they use the monsoon winds to reach India.

Medieval Inventions

After Rome's Western Empire fell in AD 476, a period known as the Dark Ages began in Europe, with few advances in learning and few inventions. The civilizations of the Arab Islamic world still flourished and in China inventors continued to break new ground.

During the early Middle Ages, as the monasteries in Europe began to explore ancient learning, and the Christian Crusaders to see the learned centres of Islam, a new culture grew and many inventions occurred.

I'VE GOT THE WHEEL, BUT HOW DO I USE THE JACK?

EUROPE

EUROPE

C. 700 Wrought-Iron Smelting from Catalonia

C. 800 'King Alfred's' Candle Clock

C. 900–1000 Wheeled Ploughs, used earlier by the Romans, become widespread

C. 1065 Stained Glass (Augsburg Cathedral)

C. 1129 Flying Buttresses, St. Denis

C. 1150 Welsh Longbow

C. 1180 Vertical Sail Windmill

C. 1200 Spinning Wheel from India

C. 1250 De Honnecourt's Screw Jack

C. 1280 Spectacles from Venice

C. 1300 Verge Escapement Clock

C. 1300 Compass Rose

C. 1350 Muzzle-Loading Cannon (first invented in China)

1450 Gutenberg's Press

WELL, WHICH WAY IS IT THEN?

MANY EUROPEAN AND ARAB 'INVENTIONS' HAD FIRST BEEN MADE

c. 984 Chiao Wei Yo invents a canal lock.

c. 1000 Ibn-al-Haitham invents the magnifying glass.

AD 1040–50 Pi-Sheng uses movable type in China.

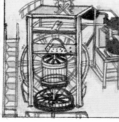

c. 725 I-Hsing makes a water clock.

c. 1150–1220 Ismaeil al-Jazari makes mechanical devices.

c. 1250 Villard de Honnecourt invents a water-powered saw.

c. 1267 The monk Roger Bacon makes lenses and gunpowder.

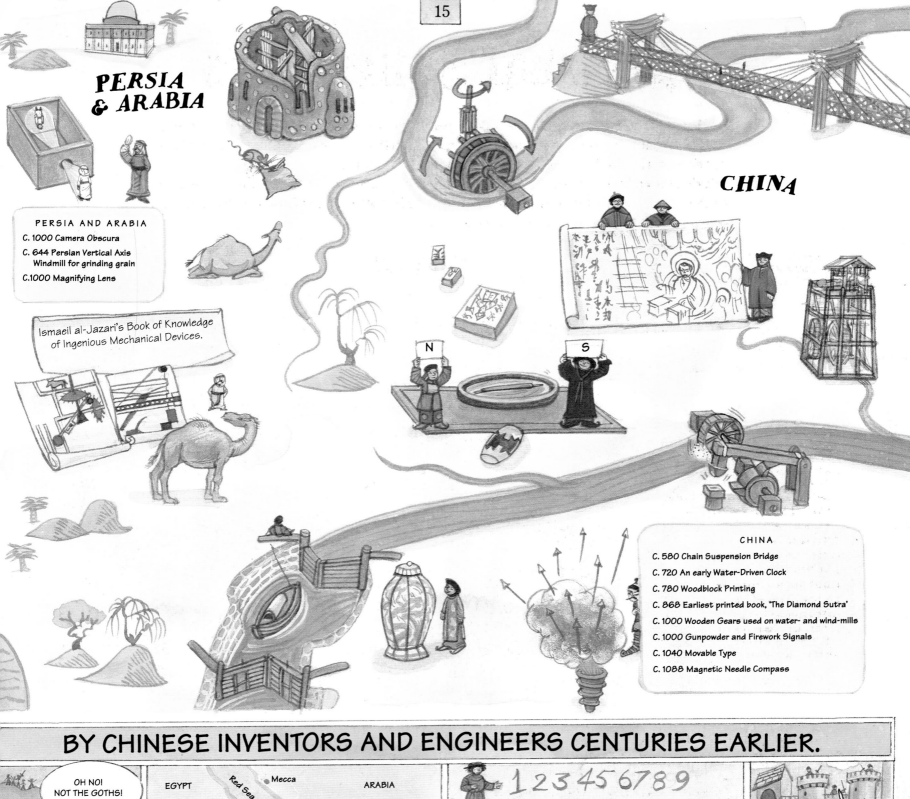

PERSIA & ARABIA

PERSIA AND ARABIA
- C. 1000 Camera Obscura
- C. 644 Persian Vertical Axis Windmill for grinding grain
- C.1000 Magnifying Lens

Ismaeil al-Jazari's Book of Knowledge of Ingenious Mechanical Devices.

CHINA

CHINA
- C. 580 Chain Suspension Bridge
- C. 720 An early Water-Driven Clock
- C. 780 Woodblock Printing
- C. 868 Earliest printed book, 'The Diamond Sutra'
- C. 1000 Wooden Gears used on water- and wind-mills
- C. 1000 Gunpowder and Firework Signals
- C. 1040 Movable Type
- C. 1088 Magnetic Needle Compass

BY CHINESE INVENTORS AND ENGINEERS CENTURIES EARLIER.

OH NO! NOT THE GOTHS!

EGYPT Red Sea Mecca ARABIA

c. 570 The prophet Mohammed is born in Mecca.

c. 960 Gerbert brings Hindu Arabic numerals to Europe.

OH NO! NOT THE TURKS!

476 Rome falls to the Goths.

1086 England's Domesday Book lists 5624 water mills.

1150-1250 Many universities are founded.

1096-1291 The Christian Crusades to the Holy Land.

c. 1320 The Aztecs found Tenochtitlan (later Mexico).

1453 Constantinople falls to the Turks.

c.1397 Johann Gutenberg 1468

Johann Gutenberg from Germany invented printing with movable type. In the early 1450s, he made mirror-image letters on movable metal type, cast the letters in his own moulds and then cut them into shape.

To prepare for printing Gutenberg put the type into sentence or type sticks, clamped them together and placed them in the printing press. The metal letters, or type, could then be changed into different combinations of words and sentences, inked up and printed many times over.

The development of printing in Europe was tremendously important. Thousands of books, hundreds of pages long, were printed, aiding the spread of ideas throughout the Western world during the Renaissance and the Reformation. Gutenberg's method of printing stayed largely unchanged until the late 20th century.

1400s Jan and Hubert van Eyck invent oil painting.

THE FIRST PRINTED BOOK, THE GUTENBERG BIBLE, APPEARED IN 1455.

A BIT SILLY TO FIGHT ABOUT ROSES.

1455 The English Wars of the Roses begin.

1453 The Turks take Constantinople, ending the Byzantine Empire.

THE RENAISSANCE

1400s A revival in music, art, architecture, literature and science begins in Italy.

1450s Under the Medici family Florence becomes a centre of Renaissance excellence.

1456 The trial of Joan of Arc is annulled.

1452 Leonardo da Vinci 1519

Leonardo was an Italian painter, sculptor, architect, engineer, man of science, writer and mathematician. He made written observations in mirror writing and hundreds of scientific and mechanical sketches and bound them together in special notebooks. They included a self-propelling car, a steam engine, a submarine, a dredger and a paddle boat, a diver's helmet, machine tools, a machine for twisting rope, and a clock.

Leonardo's interest in flight led him to sketch designs for a flapping wing and a helicopter. He studied birds, and looked at how the human body functioned, and showed how the valves in the heart worked almost 500 years before modern scientists did so. He invented the first armoured tank and designed fortifications, war machines, and canals. Many of Leonardo's ideas were centuries ahead of their time.

1514 Copernicus' theory that the earth orbits the sun is written down.

1500 Jakob Nufer delivers a baby by a Caesarian operation.

FLYING MACHINE 1 CHAIR 47 ROCKETS
BOOM

1500 In China, Wan Tu tries to build a flying machine. It explodes and Wan Tu himself is killed.

1509 Peter Henlein makes a spring-driven clockwork watch. It is known as the 'Nuremberg Egg'.

ARMOURED SHIP
TRENCH DIGGER
ASSAULT VEHICLE
FLAPPING WINGS
1486-90
HELICAL SCREW HELICOPTER
GEAR
MONA LISA
ORNITHOPTER
ANATOMICAL DRAWING
GEAR
CRANE
MAIN SPRING
DIVING MASK

LEONARDO WAS ONE OF THE WORLD'S MOST REMARKABLE INVENTORS.

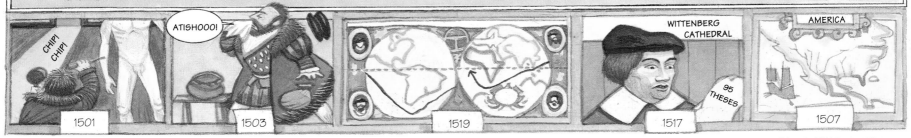

CHIPI CHIPI

1501
Michelangelo begins to sculpt his statue, David.

ATISHOOO!

1503
Pocket handkerchiefs are used in polite European society.

1519
Magellan's expedition is the first to sail around the world.

WITTENBERG CATHEDRAL
95 THESES

1517
Martin Luther protests against the Catholic Church in Germany.

AMERICA

1507
Martin Waldseemüller publishes the first maps to name America.

1512 Gerardus Mercator 1594

In 1569 Gerardus Mercator, a Flemish geographer from Belgium, invented a new system of map-making. His world map, which he drew up on eighteen sheets, was the first one ever to plot a curved surface as straight lines.

Mercator used a grid, formed by the lines of latitude and longitude, to project a globe onto a cylinder. Then he rolled his sheets out flat to make his world map. The longitudes and latitudes came out as straight lines, at right angles to one another. This new way of map-making was very important because it meant that any constant course followed by shipping over huge distances (the rhumb line) could now be plotted accurately by navigators as a straight line on his maps.

Mercator's maps helped navigators to chart the oceans and follow trade routes with far greater accuracy and safety.

SWITZERLAND
BASEL
LUCERNE
BERN

1566 Camillo Torello patents a seed drill. This is probably the first time in Europe that a seed drill is used for planting.

1565 Konrad Gesner of Switzerland invents the pencil. Its lead is made from pure graphite.

ATLAS

SOMETIMES I FEEL I'VE GOT THE WEIGHT OF THE WORLD ON MY SHOULDERS.

BOOM!

In 1585 and 1589 two parts of Mercator's great atlas are published. After his death his son publishes the third part. The atlas contains 107 maps.

WORLD MAP

I AM HERE.

1561 An early type of hand grenade is made for the first time in Europe, but the Chinese first used them c.1000 AD!

MERCATOR FIRST ISSUED THE WORD 'ATLAS' TO MEAN A BOOK OF MAPS.

1560 Jean Nicot imports the tobacco plant into Western Europe.

Tobacco contains a tar which is called nicotine.

1561 Tulips reach Western Europe from the Near East.

Plan of slave ship shows how slaves are packed together.

1562 John Hawkins begins the slave trade, shipping Africans from Guinea to the West Indies.

1565 London's Royal College of Physicians allows human dissection for the first time in England.

1561 St Basil's basilica in Moscow is completed.

1629 CHRISTIAAN HUYGENS 1695

The Dutch mathematician and astronomer, Christiaan Huygens, devised the first working pendulum clock in 1657. As it swung, the pendulum of the clock regulated the ticking. In 1675, Huygens designed another type of clock, a portable one with a balance wheel and a spiral spring oscillator.

Huygen's own lenses and telescopes led to him making many discoveries about space which included his revealing the true shape of the rings around Saturn. Later, Huygens studies gases, dynamics and light. In 1661 he invented the manometer to calculate the 'elastic' force of gases, and in 1678 he discovered the polarisation of light, and stated that light was made up of waves, not particles.

c.1650 The magic lantern is made in Germany.

1658 Hooke invents a balance spring for watches.

HUYGENS' SPRING IS NOT WORTH A FARTHING.

THE HUYGENS BALANCE SPRING

c.1650 Von Guericke invents a vacuum pump. His pump is able to suck air from a globe.

1650 Haustach of Nuremberg builds an early wheelchair

Traite de la Lumière 1690

BOTH HUYGENS AND ROBERT HOOKE CLAIMED TO HAVE INVENTED THE BALANCE SPRING.

1658 Jan Swammerdam first observes red blood corpuscles.

1657 The first stockings and fountain pens are manufactured in France.

GET OFF MY FOOT!

In 1650 the World's population is around 500 million.

1650 The first tea is drunk in England.

1651–52 Dutch Boers settle the Cape of Good Hope.

1655 Rembrandt paints a portrait of his son Titus.

1564 Galileo Galilei 1642

THE COPERNICAN UNIVERSE

THE LAW OF FALLING BODIES

1590

THE LEANING TOWER OF PISA

Venus

Saturn

Jupiter

The Moon

The Milky Way

AARGH!

c.1593 Galileo makes a thermoscope, a gas thermometer (a). Wine heated in a sealed flask is pushed up a tube as the hot air expands.

1603 Galileo's telescope (b). It is more powerful than the Lippershey telescope.

A.

B.

GALILEO TIMED THE SWING OF A PENDULUM AT PISA CATHEDRAL

1594 The French start to use hand grenades, originally a Chinese invention.

1596 Janssen invents the component microscope.

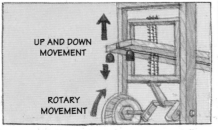

UP AND DOWN MOVEMENT

ROTARY MOVEMENT

1590s An ancient Chinese invention, the crank, starts to be widely used. It transfers rotary movement to pushing and pulling movements.

c.1590 William Lee, an English clergyman, invents the knitting machine.

1594 Davis invents the backstaff to use in navigation

1599 A two-masted land yacht first sails.

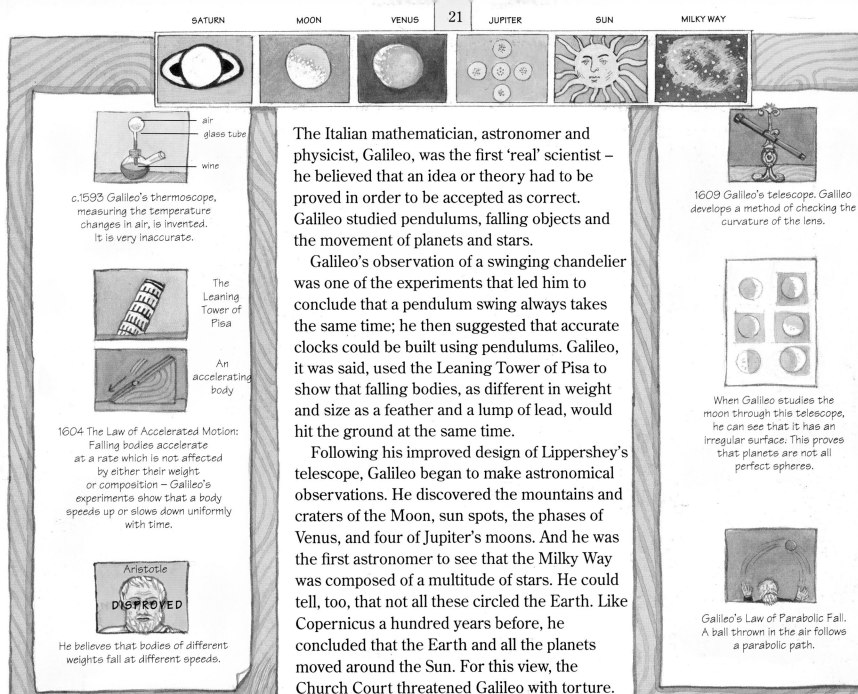

air
glass tube
wine

c.1593 Galileo's thermoscope, measuring the temperature changes in air, is invented. It is very inaccurate.

The Leaning Tower of Pisa

An accelerating body

1604 The Law of Accelerated Motion: Falling bodies accelerate at a rate which is not affected by either their weight or composition – Galileo's experiments show that a body speeds up or slows down uniformly with time.

Aristotle

DISPROVED

He believes that bodies of different weights fall at different speeds.

The Italian mathematician, astronomer and physicist, Galileo, was the first 'real' scientist – he believed that an idea or theory had to be proved in order to be accepted as correct. Galileo studied pendulums, falling objects and the movement of planets and stars.

Galileo's observation of a swinging chandelier was one of the experiments that led him to conclude that a pendulum swing always takes the same time; he then suggested that accurate clocks could be built using pendulums. Galileo, it was said, used the Leaning Tower of Pisa to show that falling bodies, as different in weight and size as a feather and a lump of lead, would hit the ground at the same time.

Following his improved design of Lippershey's telescope, Galileo began to make astronomical observations. He discovered the mountains and craters of the Moon, sun spots, the phases of Venus, and four of Jupiter's moons. And he was the first astronomer to see that the Milky Way was composed of a multitude of stars. He could tell, too, that not all these circled the Earth. Like Copernicus a hundred years before, he concluded that the Earth and all the planets moved around the Sun. For this view, the Church Court threatened Galileo with torture.

1609 Galileo's telescope. Galileo develops a method of checking the curvature of the lens.

When Galileo studies the moon through this telescope, he can see that it has an irregular surface. This proves that planets are not all perfect spheres.

Galileo's Law of Parabolic Fall. A ball thrown in the air follows a parabolic path.

BY CHECKING IT AGAINST HIS OWN PULSE.

1590 Shakespeare writes his first play, Henry VI, Parts I–III.

1591 Start of the annual custom of running bulls in the streets of Pamplona, Spain.

1592 The ruins of Pompeii are discovered.

1592 Windmills are used to drive mechanical saws in Holland.

1593 Sir Richard Hawkins recommends oranges and lemons to prevent scurvy at sea.

1623 Blaise Pascal 1662

Pascal was only eleven when he calculated the first 23 propositions of Euclid. By the age of nineteen he had made the first digital calculator, the 'Pascaline'. His calculator was operated by a system of gears and wheels and when a handle was turned it added or subtracted up to eight figures. The answers were delivered to small display windows.

Pascal's work included a theory of mathematical probability which is still used today. He continued Torricelli's work on barometric pressure and the weight of air and was a pioneer of hydraulics and pneumatics. He also set up a public transport system in Paris using horse-drawn buses.

A deeply religious man, Pascal was a philosopher as well as a mathematician. From the age of thirty-one he dedicated his life to God and wrote two famous religious books.

This barometer is the first vacuum known to science.

1643 Torricelli invents a barometer using mercury as a fluid in a sealed glass column.

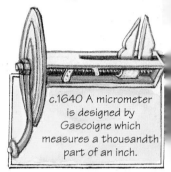

1642 Mezzotint becomes a new printing method.

c.1640 A micrometer is designed by Gascoigne which measures a thousandth part of an inch.

Puy de Dôme
Pascal's brother-in-law helped him show that air pressure balances the height of the barometer's mercury column. He took the barometer up the Puy de Dôme mountain.

TAXES

19-YEAR-OLD PASCAL MADE THE CALCULATOR TO HELP HIS FATHER WITH TAX COLLECTION.

1643 Coffee drinking becomes popular in Paris.

1640 The first European cafés open in Venice.

I THINK THEREFORE I AM

1644 Descartes writes on philosophy.

TREATY OF WESTPHALIA

1648 The end of the 30 Years War.

1618–48 The war and plague has killed 9 million Germans.

1649 Gassendi says that matter is made up of atoms.

1642 Tasman explores New Zealand and Tasmania.

1649 King Charles I of England is beheaded.

1642 Isaac Newton 1727

Isaac Newton was a mathematician, physicist, astronomer and philosopher, and his theories changed the way people looked at the world. By the time he was seventeen years old and a student at Cambridge University, Newton knew more than many of his professors, after a childhood spent reading and making scientific models.

As a young mathematics professor, Newton began to develop the rules of calculus which helped him to work out the curved path of moving objects, like the orbit of the Moon around the Earth.

Newton devised his theories on gravity on his mother's farm. There the famous apple fell on his head and set him thinking about the invisible force of attraction between objects. Newton's theory explained why the apple fell to earth when, for instance, the Moon did not fall but, instead, kept in its orbit of the Earth.

INERTIA
1. A body remains at rest or in motion at a constant speed in a straight line unless forces act upon it.

GRAVITY ACTING ON THE BODY

I AM OVERCOME BY THE GRAVITY OF THE SITUATION.

Object 1

A force acting on an object makes it accelerate. The size of the force = the mass of the object multiplied by the acceleration.

Object 2

Twice the mass = 1/2 the acceleration, if the force is the same.

3. Pairs of objects exert forces on each other.

A ⇄ B

Forces of action and reaction between A and B.

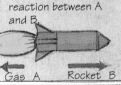

Gas A   Rocket B

Colours   White appearance

A spinning circle

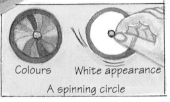

1662 Hooke invents a new improved microscope.

1660s Robert Boyle makes discoveries about gas pressure and volume.

1661

Thevenot invents the spirit level.

1666–1684 Gottfried Leibniz develops calculus independently of Isaac Newton.

1704 Newton's 'Opticks' explains that white light is made up of a 'spectrum' of bright colours.

NEWTON'S DOG 'DIAMOND' KNOCKED OVER A CANDLE AND SET FIRE TO MANY OF NEWTON'S NOTES.

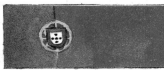

1667 Robert Boyle, author of 'The Sceptical Chemist', attempts respiration on a dog.

1666 After the 'Great Plague' the 'Great Fire' destroys large areas of London.

1668 Portugal gains independence from Spain.

1662 The Palace of Versailles is begun.

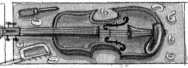

1666 Stradivari makes his first violin.

1632 Antoine van Leeuwenhoek 1723

WEIGHTED
SAFETY
VALVE

c. 1680 Denis Papin invents a pressure cooker. It is used for cooking bones.

In 1683 the Dutch merchant and naturalist, Antoine van Leeuwenhoek, invented the first accurate and powerful single lens microscope. This led to an interest in microscopic study, although he had no scientific training and was entirely self-taught.

Van Leeuwenhoek was originally a draper's apprentice and one of his tasks was to examine cloth through a magnifying glass. He started to experiment with his lenses and found a way of grinding them to make them more powerful.

After developing a number of new microscopes van Leeuwenhoek studied 'lower animals' and minute forms of life, observing the 'little animals' and recording them, without knowing exactly what these microbes were, or how they were linked with disease.

Van Leeuwenhoek's strong lenses revealed to him a new world of 'animalcules' and made microscopic study possible. His accurate descriptions of microbes formed the basis of later medical and biological research.

c. 1680 Clocks become much more accurate after William Clement and other clock makers use an improved 'anchor' escapement.

1688 The first plate glass is cast by Abraham Thevart.

Leeuwenhoek's microscope.

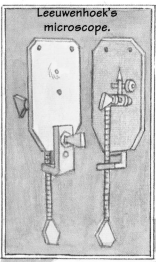

SCRATCH! SCRATCH!

BLOOD   BACTERIA   PROTOZOA   SPERMATOZOA   TISSUE   FLEA

IN 1683 VAN LEEUWENHOEK IDENTIFIES BACTERIA FROM HIS OWN TEETH SCRAPINGS.

1689 The Dutch hold the first modern trade fair in Leyden.

1680 The dodo becomes extinct.

1689 Peter the Great becomes Tsar of Russia.

1683 The last wild boar in Britain is killed.

1682 Edmund Halley observes the comet named after him.

1663 THOMAS NEWCOMEN 1729

Thomas Newcomen, a devout Christian, and Baptist preacher, made the first practical steam engine in 1712. Working as an ironmonger in England, he experimented with steam pumps to rid Cornish tin mines of water. Newcomen's invention was a genuine steam engine; it had moving parts worked by steam. This motion in turn worked the pumps.

The Newcomen engine was a pumping engine only; it could not turn shafts except by pumping water over a waterwheel. But it did reduce the cost of draining mines, and enabled deeper pits to be sunk.

1699 SAVERY'S PUMP. It was beyond the technology of the time and extremely inefficient. Newcomen co-operated with him as Savery held a patent covering raising water by fire.

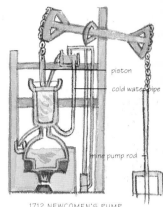

1712 NEWCOMEN'S PUMP. The actual principle of the steam engine was first demonstrated by Denis Papin c.1690.

piston
cold water pipe
mine pump rod

1714 Gabriel Fahrenheit invents the mercury thermometer. Mercury, also called quicksilver, is still used in thermometers.

1711 John Shore invents the tuning fork.

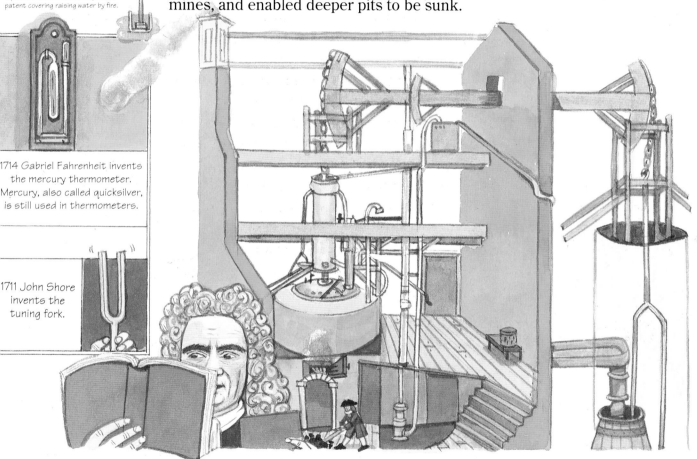

1714 The derrick, a mast-mounted ship's crane, is developed in France.

1716 Halley introduces a diving bell with an air refreshment system.

THE NEWCOMEN ENGINE SOLD SO WELL IT WAS CALLED THE 'COMMON ENGINE'.

1713 The Prussian army introduces pigtails.

1712 and 1714 Witchcraft trials are abolished in England and Prussia.

YIPPEE

c.1714 The Meissen factory in Germany starts to make porcelain.

MEISSEN FIGURES

HOORAY

1715 Vaudeville becomes popular in Paris.

BRAVO

1711 The clarinet is introduced into orchestras for the first time.

1719 Daniel Defoe writes 'Robinson Crusoe'.

1706 Benjamin Franklin 1790

Franklin's kite experiment showed that electricity produced as a flash of lightning could hit a key suspended from a kite, and travel down the kite string to the ground.

Although Benjamin Franklin, the youngest son in a family of seventeen children, spent only two years at school, he was to become a philosopher, a scientist and America's most important statesman. Franklin helped to draw up the Declaration of Independence, and the Peace Treaty in 1783 following the War of Independence. After leaving his native Boston, where he worked for his brother, a printer, Franklin moved to Philadelphia. There he founded a famous philosophical society, started a library, and organised the street lighting. In spite of his busy life Franklin found time to experiment with electricity: his dangerous kite experiment proved that lightning was a discharge of electricity. His inventions included an improved heating stove, and the first lightning conductor.

A LIGHTNING CONDUCTOR

KNOWN AS A 'FRANKLIN ROD'.

1730 Hadley invents a quadrant to measure longitude and latitude.

LIMEY!

1747 Lind proves that citrus fruit prevents the disease scurvy.

1754 the first iron-rolling mill is built in England.

1751 Baron Axel Cronstedt isolates nickel.

FRANKLIN'S BIFOCAL GLASSES

IMPROVED STOVE

DIDEROT ENCYCL

1760 Harrison perfects a marine chronometer.

1759 Brindley builds a canal aqueduct over the River Irwell in England.

1755 Joseph Black discovers the existence of carbon dioxide.

1758 Strutt invents a ribbing machine to make stockings.

FRANKLIN WAS ONE OF THE FIRST PEOPLE TO EXPERIMENT WITH ELECTRICITY

1750s Capability Brown 'improves' English landscapes.

1754 St. Petersburgh's Winter Palace is begun in Russia.

R.I.P. HANDEL

1759 The composer George Frederick Handel dies.

1759 Halley's comet returns as predicted.

1755 An earthquake in Lisbon, Portugal, kills tens of thousands of people.

1754 The first female medical doctor Dorothea Erxleben graduates in Germany.

GIVE US BACK OUR SEPTEMBER.

1752 Eleven days are 'lost' when England adopts the Gregorian calendar.

1754 George Washington leads his troops against the French in North America.

1732 Richard Arkwright 1792

In 1769 Richard Arkwright invented the 'water-frame' spinning machine which helped to bring about the Industrial Age. Arkwright's machine was much quicker than other machines and could be left to spin by itself. New factories were built to house the machines and many hand-spinners working at home were forced out of work.

Arkwright had started life in England as a barber and wigmaker, but hard work and ability helped him to leave wig-making behind him and become a mill-owner. Working long hours, he would travel at high speed between his factories in a four-horse post chaise.

On his death, Arkwright left over £500,000.

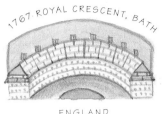
1767 ROYAL CRESCENT, BATH
ENGLAND

1760 KEW BOTANIC GARDENS
ENGLAND

1762 Roebuck invents a process to convert cast iron to malleable iron.

FIRE, FIRE!
WHO STARTED IT?

1766 Marie invents a fire escape using a basket on pulley and chains.

Arkwright's water frame was powered by water wheel. The cotton it produced was fine but strong and very good for weaving.

WATER FRAME

GOOD YARN

Spinning Machine

ARKWRIGHT
Barber   Wigmaker

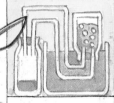
1766 Cavendish discovers the gas hydrogen.

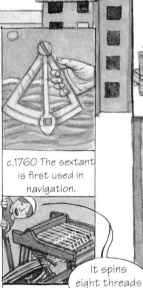
c.1760 The sextant is first used in navigation.

It spins eight threads at once.

1764 Hargreave invents the 'Spinning Jenny'.

1769 Cugnot invents the steam road carriage (the first real automobile).

I'LL WRITE AN OPERA TOMORROW

ARKWRIGHT WAS KNOWN AS THE FATHER OF THE FACTORY SYSTEM.

1768 James Cook makes his first voyage.

1760s Linnaeus' important plant and animal classifications (1759) start to be used.

1762 The flightless saltair becomes extinct.

1768 Boston citizens refuse to quarter British troops.
PUSH OFF!

1762 Rousseau writes the 'Social Contract'.

1769 Napoleon Bonaparte is born in Corsica.

1764 Eight year old Mozart writes his first symphony.

1764 House numbers are introduced in London.

1763 Pit ponies are first used in English coalmines.

1736   James Watt   1819

James Watt, the Scottish engineer, invented the first efficient steam engine at a time when the new factories of the Industrial Revolution urgently needed power.

    Watt began making his engines with Matthew Boulton. Almost every new Watt/Boulton engine saw improvements. As well as using steam, the machines used air pressure in the cylinder to make the piston work better, and 'sun and planet' gears to turn the wheels, or rotate a shaft to drive factory machinery. Watt's rotative engines enabled factories to become independent of streams and rivers, horse power and windmills. Watt also invented a governor to make sure the rotative engines worked at the constant speed necessary for driving machinery.

    When Watt wanted to describe how powerful his rotative engines were, he coined the word 'horsepower'. A '15 horsepower' engine had the same power as fifteen horses.

1769 Watt's first single-action engine.

1783 Charles flies the first hydrogen balloon.

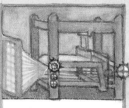
1787 Cartwright patents the 'Powered Loom'.

1784 Bramah invents a new lock – the safe and combination lock.

1784 Meikle invents the threshing machine.

1788 Miller's steam paddle boat sails at 5 knots.

C.1876 DOUBLE ACTING ENGINE

BEAM

PANTOGRAPH LINKAGE

SUN AND PLANET GEARS CONVERT UP AND DOWN MOTION TO ROUND AND ROUND MOTION.

DOUBLE ACTING STEAM CYLINDER

FIRST EVER SEPARATE CONDENSER

WATT'S WORKSHOP

JAMES WATT GAVE HIS NAME TO THE UNIT OF ELECTRICAL POWER, THE 'WATT'.

1781 American Independence as Britain's General Cornwallis surrenders at Yorktown.

1781 Herschel discovers the planet Uranus.

1780s A growing cotton industry helps to establish England's Industrial Revolution.

1788 'The Times' newspaper is founded in London.

1789 The French Revolution begins. A mob sacks the Bastille prison.

1782 Boulton's Soho Works is the first factory to be powered by a Watt Rotative Engine.

The MONTGOLFIER Brothers

Joseph
1740-1810

Jacques-Étienne
1745-1799

QUACK!

1785 Meusnier develops a lighter-than-air dirigible.

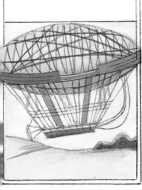

1789 Berthollet invents a chlorine gas bleach.

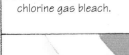
It is used for bleaching cloth.

The Montgolfier brothers, Joseph and Jacques-Étienne, made the first passenger-carrying balloons in 1783.

In the presence of King Louis XVI, at Versailles, the brothers sent the first passengers up – a cockerel, a duck and one sheep – suspended in a cage beneath the balloon. The first humans aloft were Pilâtre de Rozier and the Marquis d'Arlandes. Hanging in a basket below the balloon, they ascended over the Bois de Boulogne and drifted more than 8 kilometres across Paris in a twenty-five minute flight.

The Montgolfier balloon, made of linen and lined with paper, was 15 metres high. When the balloon was ready for flight, a fire of burning wool and straw was lit inside; as the air became hot, it lifted off into the sky.

1783 Lenormand invents a 'parachute' consisting of two parasols.

1784 Gas lamps are used to light a Paris lecture room.

We have enclosed a cloud in a bag.

THE MONTGOLFIER BROTHERS INVENTED THE HOT-AIR BALLOON.

1785 De Rozier becomes the first victim of balloon flight. The hydrogen gas catches fire over Boulogne.

1789 George Washington becomes the first president of the United States.

1788 Britain establishes a convict settlement in Australia.

1787 Balloonist Jacques Charles devises Charles' Law.

IF GAS IS HELD AT A CONSTANT PRESSURE, ITS VOLUME IS DIRECTLY PROPORTIONAL TO ITS ABSOLUTE TEMPERATURE.

1743 ANTOINE LAVOISIER 1794

Antoine Lavoisier went back to the basics of chemistry and invented the modern way of defining chemical elements. He also wrote a 'Great Treatise' on Chemistry and even helped to introduce the metric system.

Lavoisier studied the composition of air, and showed that it was a chemical reaction involving a gas he called oxygen. As well as showing the importance of oxygen for combustion, he discovered its importance in respiration.

Although Lavoisier worked for the French Revolution he was a rich and privileged man who was hated by the revolutionary leaders for having once been a royal tax collector.

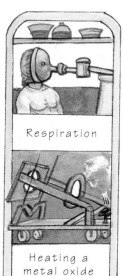

1792 Chappé's mechanical semaphore is used.

HA HA

1799 Humphry Davy organises 'hilarious' gatherings and discovers that nitrous oxide is a painkiller.

Respiration

Heating a metal oxide

Breaking water down

The metric system

1791 Galvani experiments with animal electricity.

1792 Eli Whitney invents the cotton gin to separate cotton and its seeds.

1792 Murdock makes methane gas from heated coal.

ROBESPIERRE 1794 · DANTON 1794 · CHARLOTTE CORDAY 1793 · MADAME DU BARRY 1793 · MARIE ANTOINETTE 1793 · KING LOUIS XVI 1793

EXECUTIONS

GREAT TREATISE

TABLE OF 31 CHEMICAL ELEMENTS

Antoine LAVOISIER

BONJOUR

ANTOINE LAVOISIER WAS GUILLOTINED ON 8TH MAY 1794.

KEEP OFF THE GRASS

COUP

COO!

1790 Dr Guillotin, the French physician, invents a 'humane' instrument of execution.

1791 Fleeing French royals are captured and returned to Paris.

1792 A Paris mob invades the Tuileries Gardens.

1799 Napoleon leads a coup.

1796 In the US Thomas Jefferson designs his home 'Monticello'.

1791 Joseph Haydn writes the 'Surprise' Symphony.

1799 A preserved mammoth is found in Siberia.

1792 Thomas Paine, a British radical, writes 'The Rights of Man'.

CHARLOTTE CORDAY DUNNIT

1793 Marat, the French revolutionary leader, is murdered.

1749 *EDWARD JENNER* 1823

LYMPH GLANDS

In 1796 the English physician Edward Jenner administered the first vaccination to prevent smallpox, a disease many people died from at that time. Those who did survive had faces terribly scarred by 'pockmarks'.

As a country doctor Jenner had noticed the accuracy of the old wives' tale, namely that dairy maids catching a mild disease from cows' udders, called cowpox, never seemed to catch the more serious smallpox. To test this theory, Jenner took lymph fluid from the flesh sores of a cowpox victim, Sarah Nelmes, and inserted the fluid into scratches made on the arm of an eight year old boy. The boy quickly caught cowpox and recovered.

A dose of smallpox was then put on the boy's arm in the same way but he did not catch the smallpox. The experiment was a success and Jenner became the 'father' of immunology.

VACCA IS LATIN FOR COW.

MOO!

1795 Joseph Bramah invents the hydraulic press.

1798 Aloys Senefelder invents the process of lithography.

1792 Larrey designs the first 'ambulance' to carry the wounded.

1790 Thomas Saint invents a sewing machine. (It was never developed.)

1797 Maudslay designs a small lathe which makes very accurate screw threads – used to control machine tools.

JENNER'S 'VACCINATION' WAS NAMED AFTER THE LATIN WORD FOR COW, 'VACCA'.

MINE IS VERY DOWN TO EARTH WORK.

1797 Garnerin makes the first public parachute descent from a balloon.

U.S.A. WASHINGTON

1790 Washington DC is founded.

1792 James Hoban begins work on America's White House.

VERY DENSE!

1798 Henry Cavendish discovers the mean density of the Earth.

1792 The first US dollar coins are minted.

1797 The first UK copper pennies are minted.

THE VINDICATION OF THE RIGHTS OF WOMEN

1792 Mary Wollstonecraft's book on the rights of women is published.

1745 ALESSANDRO VOLTA 1827

The Italian physicist, Alessandro Volta, discovered that contact between two different metals produces electricity. Using this knowledge, he invented the electric battery, the 'voltaic pile'. It was the first apparatus to produce a steady electric current, and the first to generate electricity using chemicals.

Volta chose to make his battery with silver coins and zinc discs, padded with wet pasteboard, building these into a pile twenty, thirty or sixty sections high. When Volta touched each end of the pile he got a shock; the bigger the pile, the greater the shock. Later, Volta improved the pile using a 'crown of cups'. A saline solution in the cups conducted the electrical current far better than wet pasteboard.

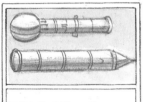

1804 Sir William Congreve develops army rockets.

THE HORIZONTAL HIGH PRESSURE ENGINE.

BOILER

c.1802 Trevithick builds a high pressure engine.

1807 Fulton's 'Clermont' is the first regular steamboat service and carries passengers along the Hudson river in America.

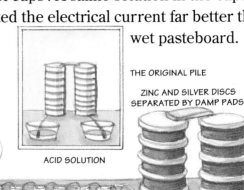

THE ORIGINAL PILE

ZINC AND SILVER DISCS SEPARATED BY DAMP PADS.

ACID SOLUTION

ZINC   SILVER   CUPS

METAL DISCS

THE FIRST ELECTRIC BATTERY

1801 Jacquard invents a loom that weaves complex designs. The loom has cards with holes punched in them. These control levers which make the designs.

MOST ELECTRIFYING, MONSIEUR VOLTA!

VOLTA DEMONSTRATED THE PILE TO NAPOLEON IN PARIS IN 1801.

1801 Piazzi discovers the first asteroid, 'Ceres'

1803-1815 The Napoleonic Wars rage in Europe and beyond.

1808 Dalton lists the elements, giving a sign and weight to each.

Element	Weight	Element	Weight
HYDROGEN	1	STRONTIAN	46
AZURE	5	BARYTES	68
CARBON	54	IRON	50
OXYGEN	7	ZINC	56
PHOSPHOROUS	9	COPPER	56
SULPHUR	13	LEAD	90
MAGNESIA	20	SILVER	190
LIME	24	GOLD	190
SODA	28	PLATINA	190
POTASH	42	MERCURY	167

1804 Beethoven dedicates his 3rd Symphony, the 'Eroica', to Napoleon.

1785 Baron von Drais von Sauerbronn 1851

Karl von Drais von Sauerbronn patented the first recognizable modern bicycle in 1817. He launched his pedal-less, wooden 'Draisienne' running-machine in Frankfurt, and in Paris. The Draisienne became popular particularly in England where an improved version, the 'hobbyhorse', was introduced in 1819. It was also copied in America.

The Draisienne was really built for amusement and was never a serious form of transport. Unlike the modern bicycle it was propelled forward by sitting in the saddle and 'walking' along the road.

1814 Maelzel invents a metronome to beat musical time.

I CAN HEAR TICKING.

1816 Laënnec invents a single tube stethoscope for listening to the heart, lungs and blood vessels.

1816 Brewster makes a kaleidoscope.

THE ART OF PRESERVING ALL KINDS OF ANIMAL & VEGETABLE SUBSTANCES

1810 Appert wins a prize for demonstrating how heat sterilization can preserve bottled food.

1815 Davy invents a safety lamp to use in coal mines.

ABOUT TIME TOO!

DEAD CANARY

SAUERBRONN'S IDEA TO INTRODUCE TWO-WHEELED TRANSPORT WAS REVOLUTIONARY.

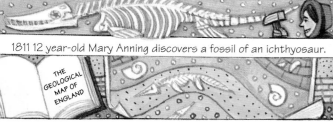

1811 12 year-old Mary Anning discovers a fossil of an ichthyosaur.

THE GEOLOGICAL MAP OF ENGLAND

1815 Smith is the first to identify rocks by fossil types.

SAY, WHERE'S OUR SUMMER GONE?

1815 An Indonesian volcano kills many thousands, and the dust fallout lowers world temperatures.

1814 British forces burn Washington D.C.

BANG

BOOM AAGH

1815 At the Battle of Waterloo, Blücher and Wellington defeat Napoleon.

WHAT WAS THAT?

1819 Beethoven goes deaf.

1792 Charles Babbage 1871

The English mathematician, Charles Babbage, invented the world's first digital computer, the mechanical 'Analytical Engine'. As a young man he made barrel organs for a hobby – these worked by pushing air through holes punched in card, blowing each pipe at precisely the moment needed to play the tune. Why not, he thought, use the same technique to produce a machine making mathematical calculations instead of musical notes? In 1822, therefore, Babbage set to work making a model calculator, the 'Difference Engine', with levers and gears. Babbage then devoted years to developing the 'Analytical Engine'. Operated by steam, and needing a coal scuttle and a watering can, this mechanical computer made arithmetical calculations, stored them in a memory, and made decisions based on the calculations. The computer was never completed and another 120 years were to pass before computers became a reality.

1827 Chemist John Walker invents the sulphur friction match.

NOW LET ME SEE, WHAT'S 2 × 7 =

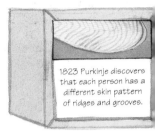
1823 Purkinje discovers that each person has a different skin pattern of ridges and grooves.

1827 Ressel invents the ship's screw propeller.
WHIRRR

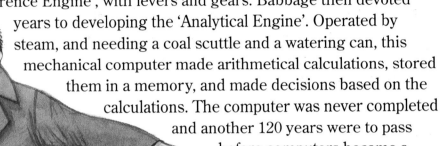

1829 Braithwaite and Ericsson build a horse-drawn steam-powered fire engine.

1827 Fourneyron and Burdin build a water turbine.

BABBAGE'S PROGRAMMABLE COMPUTER HAD THOUSANDS OF MOVING PARTS.

KEEP OUT OF OUR HEMISPHERE!

free-dom fighter
Simón Bolivar

ROAR!
BAA!

OH DEAR, WHERE WILL IT ALL END?

1823 American President Monroe issues a warning doctrine to Europeans.

1829 Hydrotherapy, treating diseases by water, is developed by Priessnitz.

1820s South American countries win freedom from Spain and Portugal.

1829 Britain's Royal Zoological Society takes over the menagerie at the Tower of London.

1822 Schubert begins his 'Unfinished' Symphony.

1766 Charles Macintosh 1843

TECHNOLOGY

1829 Bigelow invents the word 'TECHNOLOGY'.

Charles Macintosh was a Scottish chemist who invented the weatherproof fabric, the basis of the raincoat which now bears his name.

Macintosh discovered, in 1819, that India rubber would dissolve in a coal-tar product, called naphtha, and that this solution could be painted onto pieces of woollen cloth. When they were pressed together, Macintosh found that they produced a fabric which was waterproof and which could be individually tailored into a garment.

In 1830 Macintosh and his partner, Thomas Hancock, began to manufacture ready-to-wear raincoats.

MACINTOSH'S FACTORY

Macintosh's sandwich of naptha and latex between fabric.

1825 Telford's single span Menai Straits bridge is a pioneer of modern bridge construction.

1825 Chevreul and Gay-Lussac patent fatty acid candles. They are more popular than tallow candles.

1825 Appolt invents the laboratory changer gas-producing retort.

1825 Drummond invents limelight, an intense beam of focused light.

1820 Oersted discovers that electric current flowing through a wire will deflect a compass needle.

MACINTOSHES WERE CRITICISED FOR BEING SMELLY AND LOOKING LIKE SACKS!

1822 Bullock explores Mexico's Aztec ruins and brings back Aztec relics.

TEOTIHUACAN CITY

AND ABOUT TIME TOO!

1822 Champollion makes the first translation of Egyptian hieroglyphics using the famous Rosetta stone.

1835 The Catholic church removes its ban on teaching the Copernican system.

brr...

1821 Venetz says that most of Europe was once covered by glaciers.

THAT'S SILLY. THEY'LL BE SAYING THERE'S A HOLE IN THE ATMOSPHERE NEXT!

1827 Fourier says that human activities are affecting the Earth's climate.

1765 Joseph Nicéphore Niepce 1833

In 1816 the Frenchman, Joseph Nicéphore Niepce, took a picture (with a camera obscura) from his workroom window, the world's first positive photographic image. The image faded quickly.

Ten years later Niepce produced a permanent, or 'fixed', photographic image. This was the world's first photograph; once again it was a view of the rooftops seen from his attic window. The exposure took many hours and the photograph itself was dark and blurred.

A few years after his death his friend and partner, Louis Daguerre, discovered how to make sharp, clear photographs with an exposure time lasting only a few minutes. He went on to make his fortune.

TO MEASURE ELECTRIC CURRENT IN A CIRCUIT.

1820 Nobili develops the galvanometer.

PATENT No. 1
TYPEWRITER

1829 Burt is granted the first patent for a typewriter.

CAMERA OBSCURA

Silver Chloride

glass

WHITE

NIEPCE

DAGUERRE

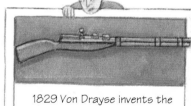

WHY SHOOT NEEDLES?

1829 Von Drayse invents the breechloading needle gun.

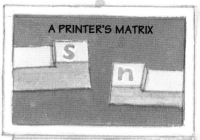

A PRINTER'S MATRIX

S

n

1829 Printer Claude Genoux invents the papier-mâché matrix.

NIEPCE'S FIRST PHOTOGRAPH HAD AN EXPOSURE TIME OF OVER 8 HOURS.

1824 The Erie canal in America is completed.

1829 A centralized Metropolitan Police force is started in London.

1829 Louis Braille invents a reading system for the blind.

1823 Brighton's Royal Pavilion is built for the English Prince Regent.

GEORGE STEPHENSON

The British engineer, George Stephenson, started work in a coal mine when he was only seven years old. Almost forty years later, in 1825, he was to see his 'Locomotive No.1' run on the first public railway. Four years later, in 1829, George and his son, Robert, built the famous 'Rocket', which was faster than any other engine.

Railways were a major 19th century invention. They enabled people to travel long distances with ease for the first time, and allowed raw materials and goods to be transported cheaply and quickly. Before the railways, long journeys had been undertaken by stage-coach, a slow, uncomfortable, and expensive way to travel.

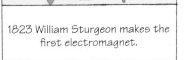

1823 William Sturgeon makes the first electromagnet.

GLASS BEAD

1828 Samuel Jones patents the Promethean match, a glass bead containing acid.

1822 Fresnel perfects lenses for light-houses.

LOCOMOTIVE NO.1

HUSKISSON'S DYING WORDS 'OWCH'.

1829 The politician Huskisson is killed at the opening of Stephenson's Liverpool to Manchester Railway.

1829 STEPHENSON'S 'ROCKET' WAS THE FIRST REALLY SUCCESSFUL STEAM ENGINE.

1824 Prévost and Dumas prove that sperm is essential for fertilization.

1828 Karl von Baer establishes the science of embryology.

L. CHAD

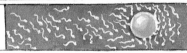

1823 Walter Oudney is the first European to see Africa's Lake Chad.

1827 Karl Baedeker publishes the first of his famous travel guides.

BAEDEKER'S GUIDE NO.1

BUT DOES IT TELL YOU HOW TO FIND LAKE CHAD?

1825 Tea roses from China are introduced into Europe.

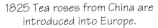

1791 SAMUEL MORSE 1872

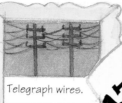

Telegraph wires.

A B C D
E F G
H I J K
L M N
O P
S
V W

Samuel Morse was a well-known American painter. During a voyage from London to New York he became fascinated by the problems of passing messages by wire. Morse set to work to solve the problem, and developed an idea for sending messages by electrical pulses along a wire. By 1832 Morse's 'electric telegraph' was in place and soon his telegraph lines were erected right across the United States.

In 1838 Morse devised a system of dots and dashes, the famous Morse Code; this allowed long and short electric signals sent along wires to be translated into letters of the alphabet. His code has since been simplified but it is still in use, especially in ship-to-shore radio communication.

1839 Charles Goodyear makes vulcanized rubber.

1834 Hansom cabs appear on the streets.

IT'S BURGLAR-PROOF!

1835 Chubb's new safe.

1837 Beer and Medler make the first accurate moon-map.

THE MORSE KEY

For transmitting the electrical code along wires

IN 1844 MORSE SENDS HIS FIRST MESSAGE WHICH READS 'WHAT HATH GOD WROUGHT'

1844 THE FIRST AMERICAN TELEGRAPH LINE BALTIMORE – WASHINGTON.

1831 Sir James Clark Ross finds the position of the North Pole.

1833 A huge shower of meteors is seen over the United States.

1833 'The Principles of Geology', Sir Charles Lyell's study of rocks, explains how gradual changes shaped the Earth.

The SS 'Royal William'

1833 The first Atlantic crossing using only steam power takes place.

1837 Sir Isaac Pitman devises shorthand.

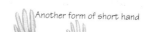

Another form of short hand

1814 SAMUEL COLT 1862

At the age of thirteen, the young Samuel Colt ran away to sea. While at sea he made his first model wooden revolver. He was still a young man when he put his hobby to practical use, developing a hand-held gun able to fire six bullets without reloading. His revolvers were used in the American Civil War and, more famously, in the Wild West.

The first revolvers had a cartridge cylinder which turned when the hammer was cocked. Although Colt patented his idea in 1835 and 1836, success came very slowly. But in 1847 the US Government ordered 1000 pistols and from then on Colt's armoury business flourished. Other work by Colt included a design for an electrically-controlled naval mine, the first to use remote control.

1835 William Fox Talbot invents the negative–positive process to make photographic images.

THE 'CALOTYPE' OF A WINDOW

The most famous Colt pistol, popular in the Wild West, was the six shot single action 'Peacemaker' model.

1830 Budding invents a lawnmower.

BANG!!

1834 Cyrus McCormick invents a reaping machine.

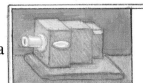

1839 Louis Daguerre devises a photographic process which makes high quality images.

The photographic plate is copper coated with silver and iodine.

'Daguerreotypomania' spreads around the world.

1835 Ada, Countess Lovelace, daughter of the poet Lord Byron, writes the first computer program.

1839 Kirkpatrick Macmillan builds the first bicycle, a velocipede.

THE 'COLT' OR 'SIX-SHOOTER' WAS THE FAVOURITE WEAPON OF BUFFALO BILL.

The 1830s see the beginning of a great era of railway-building in the United States, Britain and Europe.

1834 Both of Britain's Houses of Parliament burn down.

In the 1830s white settlers travel West and move the native Americans from their land.

1831 Slavery is abolished in the British Empire.

1791 Michael Faraday 1867

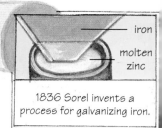
iron
molten zinc

1836 Sorel invents a process for galvanizing iron.

From humble beginnings, Michael Faraday, an English blacksmith's son, became one of the greatest pioneers of electricity and magnetism. He was a brilliant chemist as well as an outstanding experimental physicist.

In 1821, at the age of thirty, Faraday demonstrated the principle of the electric motor. Ten years later he invented the dynamo and the transformer. At the time Faraday did not realize the transformer's value or its practical use, but he was able to demonstrate that if a current in a wire wound on one side of an iron ring is interrupted, it will generate current in a second wire wrapped around the opposite side of the same ring.

Faraday was also responsible for the first lighthouse to be run by electricity. He learned, too, how to liquefy gases, including chlorine and, in 1825, he isolated benzene.

His key scientific discoveries laid the foundation for electrical engineering.

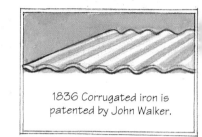

1836 Corrugated iron is patented by John Walker.

ELECTRICAL ENERGY IS CONVERTED INTO MECHANICAL ENERGY.

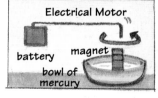
Electrical Motor
battery
magnet
bowl of mercury

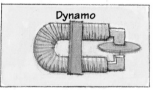
Dynamo

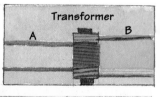
Transformer
A   B

Henry makes a dynamo at the same time as Faraday.

1831 Henry also invents an electric bell.

Fan Shaped Blades

1836 Ericsson patents a double screw propeller.

Vertical Boiler Installed

1836 Hancock makes a passenger steam road carriage.

B
A

THE FIRST TRANSFORMER – TWO COILS OF WIRE WOUND ROUND A RING.

WHILE WORKING AS A BOOKBINDER'S ERRAND BOY FARADAY TAUGHT HIMSELF SCIENCE.

1839 The first Grand National is run at Aintree, England.

1830 Joseph Smith founds the Religious Society of Mormons.

1839 Schleider and Schwann describe animal and plant cells.

PLEASE WELCOME JOYCE HETH, 160 YEARS OLD AND GEORGE WASHINGTON'S NURSE!

1835 US showman Phineas T. Barnum begins his career.

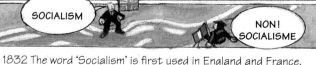
SOCIALISM
NON! SOCIALISME

1832 The word 'Socialism' is first used in England and France.

1834 Henry Blair's seed drill: the first known African-American patent.

1831 Victor Hugo writes 'The Hunchback of Notre-Dame'.

1822 ETIENNE LENOIR 1900

In about 1860 Etienne Lenoir, a self-taught Belgian-born engineer, made the first practical internal combustion engine. The Lenoir engine, based on a steam engine design, replaced steam in the cylinder with a fuel mixture of coal-gas and air, ignited by an electric spark. When the engine was started it made a terrifying noise, like a cannon firing, but as it was compact and convenient it was used in France and England for low-energy work like printing and pumping. Lenoir also worked on other inventions such as railway signals, electric motors and telegraphy.

Although a system of spark ignition is still used today Lenoir, at the time of his death, was a poor man.

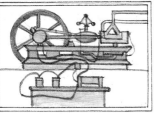

Lenoir's Gas Engine.

An explosion in the cylinder pushes forward a piston. A mixture of coal gas and air is drawn into the cylinder by the movement of the piston, and the cycle begins again.

1864 Slater invents the roller drive chain. It has many uses in industry and is still used on bicycles.

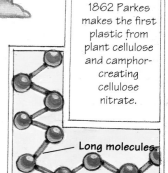

1862 Parkes makes the first plastic from plant cellulose and camphor-creating cellulose nitrate.

Long molecules.

THE CELLULOSE NITRATE STRUCTURE OF LINKED MOLECULES

1863 Butterick devises the first paper dress pattern.

1862 Louis Pasteur demonstrates that germs cause disease.

THE LENOIR ENGINE that works!

THE LENOIR ENGINE SUITABLE FOR LOW POWER USES.

1860s LENOIR'S HORSELESS CARRIAGE WAS POWERED BY AN INTERNAL COMBUSTION ENGINE.

1865 Maria Mitchel is the first woman professor of astronomy.

1864 The first salmon is canned in the United States.

1866 A meat packing factory opens in Chicago.

OH MY CAMERA!

LOVELY WEATHER!

1863 The photographer Nadar makes a balloon ascent.

1861 Daily weather forecasts begin in Britain.

1865 Edward Whymper climbs the Matterhorn.

1860s The first ships sail down the Suez Canal.

1867 The Paris fair shows Japanese art.

1806

I.K.BRUNEL

1859

1840 Sir Charles Barry begins building the Houses of Parliament in London.

1849 Nelson's Column is erected in Trafalgar Square in London.

1849 Cayley's glider first flies across a valley in England.

1845 Thomson invents the rubber tyre.

1846 Sobrero invents the explosive, nitro-glycerine.

DANGER!
NITRO-GLYCERINE

THE GREAT WESTERN

THE GREAT WESTERN

THE GREAT BRITAIN

THE GREAT BRITAIN

THE GREAT EASTERN

THE GREAT EASTERN

gear wheel

light beam

mirror

1849 Fizeau discovers a way of measuring the speed of light.

1845 Hoe patents a rotary press.

1842 Crawford W. Long uses ether to anaesthetize patients.

BRUNEL'S THREE GREAT STEAMSHIPS WERE THE LARGEST STEAMSHIPS

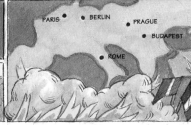

Ireland

PARIS • BERLIN • PRAGUE • BUDAPEST • ROME

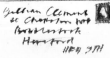

1840 Rowland Hill introduces a pre-paid penny post for letters in Britain.

1843 Charles Dickens writes his story 'A Christmas Carol'.

1846 Millions die or emigrate when a potato blight causes famine in Ireland.

1848 Revolution spreads across Europe as people seek political freedom and nationhood.

1842 Richard Owen first names two groups of prehistoric reptiles DINOSAURS.

 a penny black

1835 Brunel's broad gauge railway.

1852–1854 Brunel builds Paddington Station, London.

1841 Box Tunnel near Bath.

1837 Gooch's locomotive which Brunel acquired.

A man of enormous energy, Isambard Kingdom Brunel was one of England's greatest civil and mechanical engineers. He began his working life in 1825 helping his father, Sir Marc Isambard Brunel, build the first tunnel under the Thames. He later designed and built machines, docks, bridges, railways, stations, and even a prefabricated hospital for the Crimea.

In the 1830s Brunel designed the Clifton Suspension Bridge in Bristol. He went on to become chief engineer to the Great Western Railway and to develop the first of his highly inventive transatlantic steamers. 'The Great Western', a wooden paddle ship, was the first steamer to provide a regular transatlantic service, 'The Great Britain' was the first transatlantic screw liner. 'The Great Eastern', built in 1858 to go to Australia and back without refuelling, was the first ship with both propeller and steam propulsion and was also responsible for laying the first transatlantic telegraph cable.

Brunel also invented a machine to dislodge a sovereign coin from a windpipe.

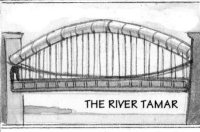

THE RIVER TAMAR

1853 The Royal Albert Bridge at Saltash is begun.

1831–64 Work on the Clifton Suspension Bridge finished after Brunel's death.

1837 The Great Western is launched

1843 The Great Britain is launched.

1858 The Great Eastern is launched.

IN THE WHOLE WORLD AT THE TIME OF THEIR LAUNCH, 1837–1858.

In 1828 Brunel was hurt when the Thames Tunnel flooded.

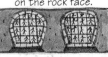

Teams of men at work on the rock face.

The revolutionary new tunnelling shield which saved the workmen from a sudden collapse of the tunnel walls.

The Brunels, father and son, work on the Thames Tunnel from 1825 to 1841.

1811 ELISHA OTIS 1861

1852 Giffard makes a large steam-powered steerable airship.

1856 Bessemer invents a steel-making process which allows it to be mass-produced.

1857 Louis Pasteur proves that fermentation is caused by living organisms.

The American manufacturer Elisha Otis's safety elevator undoubtedly made the designing and building of skyscrapers more likely. Who would have thought of designing skyscrapers without elevators safe enough to carry people up and down?

As a young man Otis made wagons and carriages, and invented labour-saving devices. In 1853 he designed a safety hoist, or elevator, with a mechanism to prevent the elevator from falling, if the attached rope or chain broke. He demonstrated his new invention by getting an assistant to cut the rope after he had ascended in the elevator.

In 1857, Otis installed the first passenger safety elevator and in 1861 he patented an elevator powered by a steam engine. During those years he was also busy designing railway wagons and brakes, a steam plough and an oven.

GOING DOWN!

1851 New modular or prefabricated building construction: Paxton's Crystal Palace.

1855 The Bunsen burner, named after Wilhelm Bunsen, is invented.

1853 Pravaz invents the hypodermic syringe.

SNIP!

KERRUNCH!

GOING DOWN!

THE OTIS STEAM ELEVATOR CO. INSTALLED THE FIRST PASSENGER LIFT IN A NEW YORK SHOP.

1851 Herman Melville's novel 'Moby Dick' is published.

1851 The Great Exhibition in London displays the world's industry and produce.

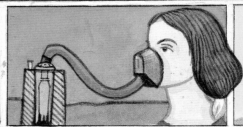

1853 Chloroform, used for childbirth, is popularized by Queen Victoria.

1854 US Commodore Perry forces Japan to sign a treaty to trade with America.

1819 EDWIN DRAKE 1880

The American, Edwin Drake, drilled the first productive oil well.

Drake started his career as a railway conductor in Connecticut, but after the value of oil had been recognized in the 1830s, Drake bought stock in the Pennsylvania Rock Oil Company and set about learning salt-well drilling. In 1858 Drake started drilling for oil at Titusville, Pennsylvania, using a steam engine to drive his metal drilling tool. Three months later he struck oil at 21 metres and soon the well was yielding 40 barrels a day.

Drake's invention spread like wildfire, creating oil boom towns in NW Pennsylvania. But he had failed to patent his oil drill, and was to live in poverty for ten years until the Pennsylvania legislature awarded him a state pension.

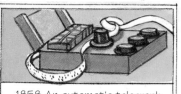
1858 An automatic telegraph system is invented by Wheatstone.

1856 Mauvine is the first synthetic aniline dye to become available. In 1859 magenta dye becomes available.

1858 The first 'workable' translatlantic telegraph cable is laid between Ireland and Newfoundland.

NEWFOUNDLAND

IRELAND

1855 Lundstrom's new safety match first gains recognition.

DOVER

CALAIS

1850 The first underwater telegraph cable is laid between Dover in the south of England and Calais in the north of France.

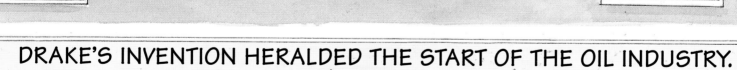

DRAKE'S INVENTION HERALDED THE START OF THE OIL INDUSTRY.

ALPS
1853 The first railway is built through the Alps.

1855 Florence Nightingale reforms nursing during the Crimean War.

USA
1852 The United States imports sparrows to control caterpillars.

1852 Mathysen, an army surgeon, stiffens bandages with plaster.

OOPS
1859 Charles Blondin crosses Niagara Falls on a tightrope.

1833 Alfred ✦ Nobel 1896

PHYSICS · CHEMISTRY · NOBEL · MEDICINE · PRIZES · PEACE · LITERATURE

TO MASS-PRODUCE TOOLS ACCURATELY

1862 Brown invents the universal milling machine.

1868 Maughan designs a water heater which uses a gas burner.

Alfred Nobel was a brilliant young chemist who, at the age of sixteen, was sent to study in Paris and America. After Nobel returned to his native Sweden his younger brother, Emil, and four others were killed in his nitro-glycerine factory.

Following that tragedy Nobel devoted his energies to devising a 'safer' explosive, 'dynamite', for use in engineering. Ten years later, in 1876, he developed the more powerful 'gelignite'. His inventions were used for military purposes which Nobel disliked and with his fortune he founded the famous Nobel Prizes for physics, chemistry, literature, physiology and medicine, and peace.

NITRO-GLYCERINE

WOOD PULP

SODIUM NITRATE

1866 Winchester invents a repeating rifle with a 'volcanic action' lever.

HOT GAS AIR
MOLTEN METAL

1864 Siemens and Martins invent an open hearth steel-making process.

1864 Mendel uses peas to investigate laws of heredity.

NOBEL LEFT HIS FORTUNE TO ESTABLISH ANNUAL PRIZES FOR EXCELLENCE.

1861–65 The American Civil War takes place between the Union and Confederate states.

1861 A fossilized Archaeopteryx is found in Germany.

It is the link between a bird and a reptile.

1862 Otto von Bismarck becomes Prussia's Prime Minister.

1864 Dunant founds the International Red Cross.

1865 The Salvation Army is founded by William Booth.

1827 Joseph Lister 1912

In 1867 the English surgeon and medical scientist, Joseph Lister, devised an antiseptic for surgical operations. The introduction of general anaesthetics in 1846 had meant that people could at last be operated on painlessly, but within days or weeks half of them died from infection. This was known as 'hospital disease'.

Pasteur's germ theory showed Lister that bacteria, breeding in the open wounds, caused the deadly infections. Lister looked for a solution which would kill the bacteria without killing people. He chose carbolic acid, at that time used to clean sewers and drains. His success was dramatic, with both his 'antiseptic', and his introduction of white operating garments, greatly reducing infection during surgery and saving countless lives.

1868 A traffic light is introduced in London using only red and green lights for the first time.

1866 Whitehead designs the first underwater missile, or torpedo.

1865 Hyatt invents celluloid (an early plastic) billiard balls. Until then all billiard balls were made from ivory.

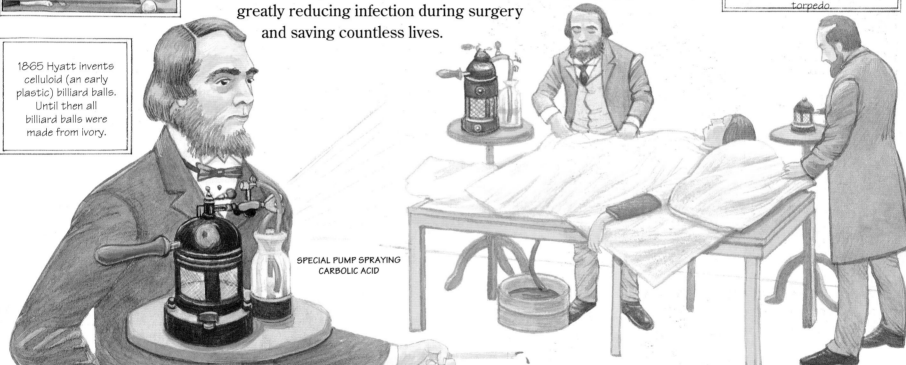

SPECIAL PUMP SPRAYING CARBOLIC ACID

EVEN IN LISTER'S TIME SURGEONS OPERATED IN OLD AND DIRTY CLOTHES.

1865 Lewis Carroll writes 'Alice's Adventures in Wonderland'.

PIPELINE

1865 The first oil pipeline was laid in Pennsylvania.

WE CAME AFTER THE NEANDERTHAL PEOPLE.

1868 A skeleton of Cro-Magnon man is found in France.

SPASIBA

1867 Russia sells Alaska to the United States for $7,200,000.

1869 The Meiji open Japan to foreign trade.

1847 THOMAS EDISON 1931

RECORDING SOUND

ELECTRICAL GENERATOR

EARLY PHONOGRAPHS

1912 EDISON OPERA CONCERT PHONOGRAPH

KINETO-SCOPE

GOOD MORNING!

PLAYING BACK

VOTING MACHINE

35mm CELLULOID

THE FIRST RECORD EVER MADE WAS OF EDISON RECITING 'MARY HAD A LITTLE LAMB'.

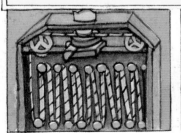

1891 The Kinetoscope.   1879 The Incandescent Lamp.   1879 The Phonograph.   1879 The Telephone.   1870 The Stock Market Ticker.

HALLO, HALLO!
with these words Edison tested his phonograph to see if it could both record and play back sounds. His phonograph separated the parts of the machine for recording and for playing back sound. People bought the phonographs for playing music and for recording conversations.

STEEL RIBS

Thomas Edison was one of the world's most successful inventors and his inventions were to revolutionize life in the twentieth century. As a boy he spent only a few months at school before starting work as a railway newsboy at the age of twelve; he even printed his own newspaper on the train.

The first of Edison's inventions were a repeating telegraph, which saved time on retapping messages, and a telegraphic printer.

In 1877 Edison made practical improvements to Bell's telephone and in 1879 he invented the first machine to record sound and play it back. He called it the phonograph. During that period he also introduced his most famous invention – the incandescent carbon filament light bulb.

Another of Edison's major achievements was the kinetoscope. This was the first film projector to produce a moving picture, and marked an important step in the development of America's motion picture industry.

Edison established the first industrial research laboratory. He called his laboratory an 'invention-factory'.

EDISON'S MENLO PARK LABORATORY

1873 Glidden's barbed wire means that cheap fencing becomes available.

1876 The Plimsoll line on ships' hulls shows the safe loading level.

1875 Otto's 4-stroke internal combustion engine.

1876 Bissell's carpet sweeper.
ROTATING BRUSH

EDISON RECORDS ALL OVER WORLD

1874 Fox's steel umbrella.

1859 Planté's battery. It contains lead-acid and is rechargeable.

1874 Sholes' type First made by Remington.

1870 Starley's Penny Farthing bicycle.

EDISON PATENTED OVER A THOUSAND INVENTIONS DURING HIS LONG CAREER.

1874 Riveted jeans made by Levi Strauss.

1879 The Tay Bridge disaster takes place in Scotland.

1870 Rome becomes the capital of recently united Italy.

1871 Charles Darwin writes 'The Descent of Man'.

1875 Roller skating becomes popular.

1871 Jules Verne writes 'Around the World in 80 Days'.

1847 Alexander Graham Bell 1922

After leaving his native Scotland Alexander Graham Bell, who came from a family of speech therapists, opened a school near Boston to teach speech to deaf people. One day Bell's assistant was testing microphones and receivers when he accidentally plucked at a wire. Bell, working in the next room, heard the noise clearly and wondered if speech could travel down the wire in the same way. And so he started to experiment.

In 1875 Bell developed the 'multiple telegraph' ('far-writing'). In 1876 he invented the telephone ('far-voice') making it possible to operate a telephone between New York and Boston.

Bell continued with experiments to transmit sound on a beam of light, and with sound recording. He also invented a kite large enough to carry people, and a hydrofoil boat, and invested the money he made from his inventions in research into deafness.

1872 Pullman designs dining cars for trains.

THEY WORK!
1872 George Westinghouse's air-brake is first used.

1878 De Laval invents the cream separator or centrifuge.

1877 Ball bearings start to be used in bicycles.

1874 Solomon uses pressure cooking for canning foods.

1879 James Ritty invents the cash register. RING! RING!

Inventor Lewis Latimer, the son of an escaped slave, executes the patent drawings for many of Bell's telephones.

MR WATSON! COME HERE, I WANT YOU!

The urgent first words transmitted when Bell accidentally spills battery acid on his trousers.

BELL USED HIS KNOWLEDGE OF HOW THE EAR WORKS TO CARRY OUT HIS EXPERIMENTS.

1871 'Dr Livingstone, I presume.' Stanley meets Livingstone in Africa.

1871 Fire overpowers Chicago.
Jane Wells observes that babies do not sit still in seats.
1872 Jane Wells patents her Baby Jumper.

1872 The first international football (soccer) game, England v Scotland.

1875 Giles crosses Australia.
THE REAL McCOY!
1870s Elijah McCoy's lubrication devices prevent trains from overheating.

1877 Schiaparelli discovers a network of 'canali' on Mars.

G D
1834-1900

KARL BENZ &
GOTTLIEB DAIMLER

K B
1844-1929

In 1885 the German engineer Karl Benz invented the practical motor car. His three-wheeled 'Motorwagen' was the first successful petrol-engined car. In the same year the mechanical engineer Gottlieb Daimler patented an internal combustion engine to run on petrol, but he fitted his engine to a wooden bicycle. A year later Daimler was to build his first car, a 'horseless carriage' with a high-speed engine fitted to an old-fashioned coach. It proved to be more popular than Benz's properly designed but costly, and slower, motor-car.

Bertha Benz, the wife of Karl, was to make the first long-distance motor-tour. In 1888 she set off with her two teenage sons to visit relatives 180km away, having left a note for her husband telling him of their plans. After an adventurous and somewhat dangerous journey in the three-wheeler 'Motorwagen' Bertha Benz and her sons arrived safely at their destination.

Monotype

1887 Lanston patents the monotype typesetting machine. Each letter is cast separately.

1884 Lockrum Blue's corn sheller, the first of the new devices patented by African Americans following the American Civil War.

1882 Writer Adeline D.T. Whitney patents her alphabet blocks with raised letters.

1889 Anna Breadin patents her 'noiseless' school desk.

DAIMLER'S 1886 HORSELESS CARRIAGE.

WOODEN BICYCLE

BENZ'S 1885 MOTOR THREE-WHEEL 'MOTORWAGEN'

THE BENZ AND DAIMLER CAR MANUFACTURING COMPANIES MERGED IN 1926.

GIVE ME YOUR TIRED, YOUR POOR, YOUR HUDDLED MASSES . . .

1886 The Statue of Liberty is dedicated.

1885 Galton discovers finger prints.

1887 Sherlock Holmes first appears in a Conan Doyle story.

ALL MINE!

NO, NO, IT'S MINE NOW!

I WANT A BIG SHARE!

I LIVE HERE!

1884–85 The scramble for Africa begins.

ESPERANTO

1887 A universal language is invented.

I'M THIRSTY!

1887 Dr. John Pemberton invents the tonic drink Coca-Cola.

EEK!

1887–89 Paris. The Eiffel Tower is designed for the Paris Exhibition.

AUGUSTE
1862–1954

LOUIS
1864–1948

The Lumière Brothers

The French Lumière brothers, Auguste and Louis, developed the cinematograph ('movement painter') motion picture camera and used it, in 1895, to make and show the first film to a public audience.

Auguste and Louis were the sons of a painter turned photographer. When he was eighteen Louis, the younger brother, opened a factory making photographic plates. Influenced by Edison's kinetoscope, the brothers designed their cinematographs and, with their trained cameramen, made forty films – French day-to-day life, news-reels, documentaries and short comedy pieces. They travelled to cities around the world to show their popular films.

OOPS!

1892 The engineer Rudolf Diesel patents the internal combustion engine.

1894 Reno invents the escalator.

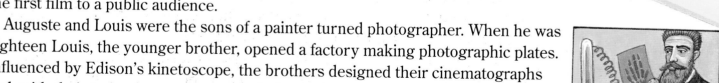

The Lumière Cinematograph

1890s Roentgen invents X-ray apparatus.

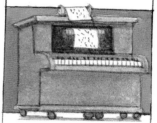

1890s Dewar invents the vacuum flask.

1897 Votey develops the pianola which plays using perforated paper.

1898 Photographs are now taken using artificial light.

THE FIRST LUMIÈRE FILM, SHOWING A TRAIN ENTERING A STATION, TERRIFIED THE VIEWERS.

QUICK NURSE, SCALPEL.

DEPTFORD

1890 England's first large-scale electrical power station is opened.

1892 Pineapples are preserved in cans for the first time.

1890 Rubber gloves are first used in surgery.

1899 The first bottles of aspirin are sold in shops.

1894 Kipling writes 'The Jungle Book'.

The Wright Brothers

Wilbur 1867-1912

Orville 1871-1948

The Wright brothers were among the greatest pioneers of aviation. They first started experimenting with kites and gliders in the mid-1890s. In 1903, at Kitty Hawk, North Carolina, Orville Wright flew 852 feet in 59 seconds in the first powered aeroplane, the first Wright Flyer. On later flights, in the United States, and France, they greatly improved on this distance.

The Wright brothers also invented the first practical aeroplane, the 1905 'Flyer III', which could fly in a circle and stay in the air for as long as thirty minutes. It could also make repeated take-offs and landings.

In 1909 they set up a company to build planes, but Wilbur died only three years later of typhoid fever.

1907 Cornu makes first free flight in a helicopter.

NOT BEFORE TIME

1901 Alva J. Fisher makes the first electric washing machine.

1902 Marie Curie finally establishes the atomic weight of radium.

HI ORVILLE!

HO WILBUR!

1900 Zeppelin flies his airship.

1909 Bleriot crosses the Channel in a plane.

1908 Henry Ford mass-produces 'Model T'.

IN 1903 ORVILLE WRIGHT BECAME THE FIRST MAN TO FLY ABOARD A POWERED MACHINE.

WE ARE NOT ALIVE

1901 Queen Victoria dies.

1907 The Cubist paintings of Picasso and Braque.

ROAR!

1903 Teddy bears appear in the US and Germany.

MONTANA

1908 A fossilized Tyrannosaurus rex is found.

VOTES FOR WOMEN

1900s Suffragettes demand women's rights to vote.

1874 Guglielmo Marconi 1937

Guglielmo Marconi, the Italian physicist and electrical engineer, invented wireless ('messages using no wires') communication and the radio.

As a young man Marconi was excited to learn of the speed at which electromagnetic waves travel through space – 300,000 kilometres per second – and wondered whether these waves could be used to send messages. Setting to work at his attic table he made his great breakthrough by the age of twenty-one, achieving the first link via radio signal. The link covered just 2.4 kilometres, with his brother firing a gun to let Marconi know that the message had been received.

By 1901 Marconi was in a position to send the first radio signals across the Atlantic, between England and Newfoundland.

1904 Fleming uses a diode (the earliest and simplest type of electronic valve) to detect radio waves.

1906 De Forest invents the triode valve. It is used mainly as an amplifier or oscillator.

1903 Poulsen makes a magnetic recorder 5 years after inventing the magnetic recording of speech.

SURPRISE FOR CRIPPEN ARREST EXPECTED

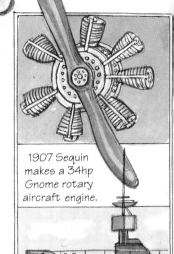

1907 Sequin makes a 34hp Gnome rotary aircraft engine.

1901 Unterseeboots, (undersea boats), known as 'U-Boats', are developed for the German navy. These submarines are used in World Wars I and II.

1907 Hoover buys Spangler's patent for a vacuum cleaner. Soon vacuum cleaners become known as 'Hoovers'.

FOR THE FIRST TRANSATLANTIC RADIO SIGNAL MARCONI TAPPED OUT 'S' IN MORSE.

CRIPPEN ARRESTED AFTER WIRELESS MESSAGE

1910 The murderer Henry Crippen is the first criminal arrested with the help of radio.

1904 Steerage rate tickets cost only $10 for migrants to the United States.

1902 A volcanic eruption and fire destroy St. Pierre, Martinique.

BEEP! BEEP!

1903 The top speed limit in Britain is only 20 mph.

1900 Freud writes 'The Interpretation of Dreams'.

1857 Konstantin Tsiolkovsky 1935

Konstantin Tsiolkovsky's fascination with flight and the exploration of space began after he caught scarlet fever as a child. The illness left him deaf and to overcome loneliness the nine year old boy taught himself mathematics and physics.

Tsiolkovsky became a teacher, but remained fascinated by space and flight. He designed bird-like gliders and metal balloon dirigibles and wrote a book called 'Dreams of Earth and Sky'. He understood that the rocket was the only means of propulsion that would work in the vacuum of space and his 1903 book, 'The Exploration of Cosmic Space by Rocket', predicted that liquid fuelled rockets could reach outer space.

In 1957, one hundred years after Konstantin Tsiolkovsky's birth, the USSR was ready at last to send up its first satellite – Sputnik I.

The EXPLORATION of COSMIC SPACE by ROCKET

1902 Bosch invents the high-tension magneto which generates electricity for the spark of the spark plug.

Original fan-shaped windscreen wiper

1903 Mary Anderson invents the first patented windscreen wiper.

IT WON'T STAIN OR RUST!

1904 Guillet invents stainless steel.

1900 Florence Parpart invents a street cleaner.

1901 Herbert Booth invents the first vacuum cleaner.

1909 Baekeland invents 'Bakelite'. It is the dawn of the PLASTIC AGE.

KONSTANTIN TSIOLKOVSKY HAS BEEN CALLED THE FATHER OF SPACE.

1902–3 Rutherford and Soddy say that atomic nuclei split to form other elements, emitting radioactivity.

1903 Sutton puts forward the chromosome theory of heredity.

1902 Heaviside and Kennelly predict that the IONOSPHERE exists, and Teisserenc de Bort discovers the troposphere and stratosphere.

LAYERS OF ATMOSPHERE

1901 The okapi is discovered in Africa.

1900s The 'Fauves' (Wild Beasts) shake up the art world.

AAAGH A RED TREE!

1908 Fountain pens start to become popular.

1906 Hopkins discovers essential nutritional foods, later named VITAMINS.

1905 The first neon light signs are seen.

1879 Albert Einstein 1955

IT DETECTS RADIATION.

BEEP BEEP BEEP

1913 Geiger invents the geiger-counter.

PROTON

1910 Rutherford discovers the proton ...

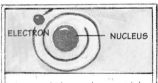

ELECTRON — NUCLEUS

... and the nuclear model of the atom.

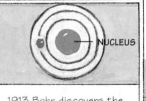

NUCLEUS

1913 Bohr discovers the structure of the atom.

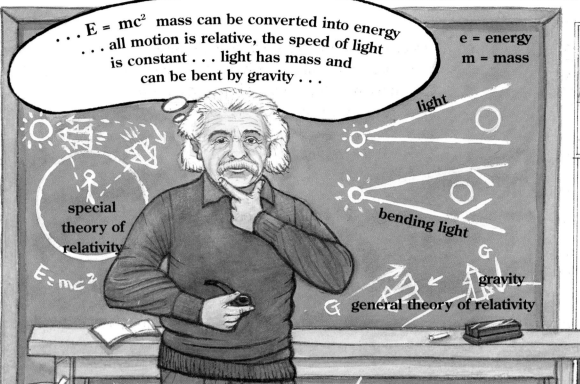

. . . E = mc² mass can be converted into energy . . . all motion is relative, the speed of light is constant . . . light has mass and can be bent by gravity . . .

e = energy
m = mass

light

special theory of relativity

bending light

$E = mc^2$

gravity

general theory of relativity

G

Max Planck

1914 Swinton develops the 'tank'.

1913 Langmuir invents the tungsten filament light.

1913 Mary Crosby makes the first brassière out of two silk handkerchiefs joined with ribbon.

1917 Clarence Birdseye experiments with food freezing.

EINSTEIN'S THEORIES OF RELATIVITY CHANGED THE WAY PHYSICISTS THOUGHT

1914 Austria's Archduke Ferdinand and his wife are assassinated in Sarajevo, sparking off World War I (1914–1918).

Much of the war is fought in trenches. Millions of soldiers die.

1912 Captain Scott and four companions die in the Antarctic after reaching the South Pole.

1912 The Titanic sinks on its maiden voyage. Over 1500 people drown.

1913 The first crossword appears in a New York newspaper.

1917 Lenin leads the Bolsheviks in the Russian Revolution.

HELP!

1911 Leonardo's 'Mona Lisa' is stolen from the Louvre in Paris.

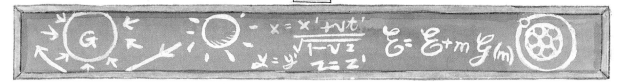

1921

There are four known fundamental forces, or 'interactions'.

ALL UNIFORM MOTION IS RELATIVE, AND THE SPEED OF LIGHT IS ALWAYS CONSTANT.

The Special Theory of Relativity

1905

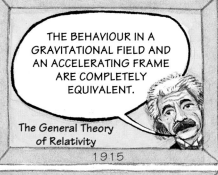

THE BEHAVIOUR IN A GRAVITATIONAL FIELD AND AN ACCELERATING FRAME ARE COMPLETELY EQUIVALENT.

The General Theory of Relativity

1915

QUANTUM THEORY SHOWS THAT LIGHT CAN MAKE ELECTRICAL ENERGY FROM SOME ELEMENTS.

Planck's Quantum Theory

1905

Einstein was the most brilliant mathematician and creative scientific mind of the 20th century. His ideas about the nature of light, space and time led to the theories of relativity and changed some of Newton's concepts of the universe, particularly gravitational theory.

Born in Germany, Einstein became a Swiss citizen in 1910 and an American citizen in 1940. In 1905 he used Planck's Quantum Theory to show how light could make electrical energy in some elements. In the same year he created a scientific sensation with his Special Theory of Relativity, which showed that the speed of light cannot be exceeded. Ten years later, in 1915, Einstein's General Theory of Relativity demonstrated that light passing a heavenly body is bent by its gravitational pull. And it was Einstein who discovered how nuclear power works – how an atom of an element losing mass can convert this mass into a huge amount of energy.

Einstein made the greatest scientific advances since Newton, 200 years before, and his theories inspired one of the major inventions of the 20th century, nuclear power.

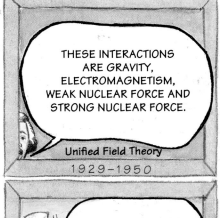

THESE INTERACTIONS ARE GRAVITY, ELECTROMAGNETISM, WEAK NUCLEAR FORCE AND STRONG NUCLEAR FORCE.

Unified Field Theory

1929–1950

THE IRREGULAR MOVEMENT OF TINY PARTICLES IN FLUIDS, DUE TO MOLECULAR BOMBARDMENT.

Brownian Movement

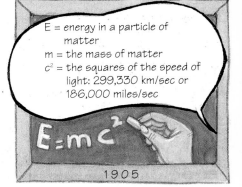

E = energy in a particle of matter
m = the mass of matter
c^2 = the squares of the speed of light: 299,330 km/sec or 186,000 miles/sec

$E=mc^2$

1905

BECAUSE THEY CONTRADICTED SOME OF NEWTON'S LAWS MADE CENTURIES BEFORE.

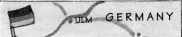
ULM GERMANY

Einstein disliked school but during his schooldays he read as much as he could.

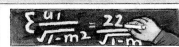
ZURICH BERNE

U.S.A.

Einstein was born in Germany, moved to Switzerland in the 1890s, and finally settled in America when Hitler came to power.

1913 Gandhi arrested in South Africa for resistance to immigration laws. He returns to India in 1915.

1910 Halley's comet makes its closest approach to the Earth.

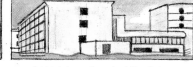
1914 Walter Gropius' Bauhaus School makes changes in architectural and arts teaching.

1917 Protesting American suffragettes are arrested for picketing the White House.

ME TARZAN
1914 Edgar Rice Burroughs writes the first Tarzan story.

1888 JOHN LOGIE BAIRD 1946

Inspired by the work of Marconi, the Scottish engineer John Logie Baird decided to experiment with sending pictures, as well as sounds, by radio waves. He set up his apparatus in an attic workshop – consisting of a tea chest, the lenses from a number of bicycle lamps, darning needles, wood, string and other bits and pieces. With this amazing apparatus he managed to transmit the fuzzy image of a cross to a receiver in the same room. A year later, in 1926, Baird was able to televise moving objects.

In 1927 Baird sent televised pictures down a telephone cable between Glasgow and London and a year later he was the first person to transmit a picture across the Atlantic.

1920 Howard invents the first Rotavator, a steam rotary hoe.

1926 Tourneau invents the first bulldozer.

HEIGHT REACHED 56M.

SPEED 97K/H.

1926 Goddard uses liquid rocket fuel (petrol and liquid oxygen) to launch his first rocket in America.

ICONOSCOPE CAMERA TUBE

1925 Zworykin produces an iconoscope in order to make an electronic transmitter, or television camera.

1920s Aerosols, cellulose tape, aerial crop spraying, hairdryers are invented.

Logie Baird's disc televisor of the 1930's, the first mass market transmitter.

BAIRD'S 1925/6 EXPERIMENTAL TELEVISION TRANSMITTER.

A disc televisor picture using a Nipkow disc invented in 1884.

1925 JOHN LOGIE BAIRD WAS THE FIRST MAN TO TRANSMIT A TELEVISION PICTURE BY RADIO WAVES.

1921 Playwright Karl Câpek coins the word ROBOT.

1920s Modernist architecture and the new international style.

I'M RUINED!

1929 The Wall Street stockmarket crash.

A 'COSMIC EGG' OF CONCENTRATED MATTER AND ENERGY EXPLODES.

1927 The first BIG BANG theory. Le Maître says that the universe began with an explosion.

1924 Lenin, who led the Russian Revolution, dies.

MY MA-A-AMMY

1923 Soundtracks on films. 'The Jazz Singer' is the first American 'talkie'.

1920 The US government passes a law to ban alcohol, beginning the 'Prohibition'.

1900 Laszlo Biro 1985

Laszlo Biro gave his name to his 1938 invention, the ball-point pen. While working as a journalist in Budapest, Biro saw magazine printers using a quick-drying ink. This gave the former painter and sculptor the idea of trying to produce a quick-drying pen. Soon afterwards he was forced to flee Hungary, ahead of a threatened Nazi invasion. In exile, in Argentina, he and his brother, Georg, continued to develop his pen.

Biro's ball-point was soon taken up by the British RAF whose crews used it for navigational calculations; it did not leak like a fountain pen even with the changes flying made to air pressure and altitude. It became a huge success and now hundreds of millions of 'biros' are sold each year.

1931 The Empire State Building is finished in New York. 102 storeys 381 metres

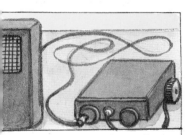

1930s The tape recorder, using magnetized plastic tape, is developed by AEG.

1935 Stevens invents the first electronic hearing aid.

1935 Magee invents the parking meter for Oklahoma City.

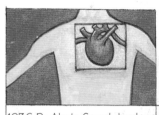

1936 Dr Alexis Carrel develops an artificial heart.

YOU HAVEN'T SEEN MY PEN, HAVE YOU?

1934 Shaw invents 'cat's eyes' glass studs to reflect car headlights in the road.

BIRO'S PEN WAS POPULAR WITH BRITISH AND AMERICAN TROOPS IN WORLD WAR II.

1930 Beebe and Barton dive 412 metres in their bathysphere.

1930 Photo flash bulbs are first used.

SO EASY FOR TOASTING!

1930 Sliced bread is introduced.

1937 The Hindenburg airship disaster in America ends the Airship Age.

1933 The film 'King Kong' is released.

1936 Hitler and Mussolini declare a Berlin-Rome axis.

1935 Stalin stages show trials against so-called traitors in Russia.

1907 FRANK WHITTLE 1996

The English aviator and engineer, Frank Whittle, built the first jet engine. The jet engine was also independently built in Germany by Von Ohain.

Whittle was only twenty-three years old when, in 1930, he registered his patent. At first, the British government were not interested and so, in 1934, Whittle set up his own company, know as 'Power Jets', to develop his engine.

By 1937 Frank Whittle's engine was ready to be tested and this time the British government gave him their support. For by now there were fears of approaching war, and of the rival German engine, the S3b. The Heinkel aircraft with the S3b engine installed actually flew first, in August 1939, just before the outbreak of war.

In May 1941 the Gloster E 28/29 flew at last with Whittle's turbo jet engine.

1931 Ruska and Knoll develop an electron microscope. The microscope is improved by Zworykin in 1939.

1937 Carlson invents the process of photocopying (xerography).

1935 Watson-Watt develops a method of detecting the position of a distant moving object: radio detection and ranging (RADAR). Soon it is used to give early warning of enemy aircraft.

MAIN ROTOR   TAIL ROTOR

1939 Sikorsky builds the first motor powered helicopter.

NYLONS 1939   NYLON FIBRES   CAROTHERS

1935 Carothers develops nylon, to be used as a man-made fabric.

WHAT'S THAT DREADFUL RACKET?

MODERN JET ENGINES ARE MODELLED ON WHITTLE'S JET ENGINE.

1932 Cockcroft and Walton split the atom.

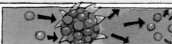
1939 Nuclear fission is discovered by Otto Hahn.

1930 Pluto is discovered by Tombaugh.

1933 Hitler becomes the German Chancellor.

1930 Amy Johnson flies solo, London-Australia.

FIRST USED ON AN AMERICAN INDIAN SITE.
1930 Douglas discovers dendrochronolgy – a dating method using tree-rings.

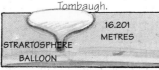
STRARTOSPHERE BALLOON   16.201 METRES
1932 Piccard establishes an altitude record.

1936 Around the world each week 250 million people watch the cinema.

1907 1980 Mauchly & Eckert 1919 1995

In 1946 two University of Pennsylvania engineers, John Presper Eckert and John William Mauchly, co-invented the first general purpose electronic digital computer.

The ENIAC (Electronic Numerical Integrator and Computer) meant that the US army could speedily calculate its artillery firing charts, by reducing calculation time from one year to around two hours. The vast ENIAC weighed nearly 30 tonnes. Its 18,000 electronic valves needed so much electricity that lights in a local town dimmed when it was in use.

After ENIAC they introduced EDVAC (The Electronic Discrete Variable Automatic Computer) which was a computer capable of changing stored instructions and altering its own programme followed in 1951 by UNIVAC (The Universal Automatic Computer) for use in business. The Computer Age was born.

1941 Zuse invents the first computer with electromagnetic relays and punched tape for data entering.

1943 Turing and others develop an electronic calculating device to crack wartime German codes.

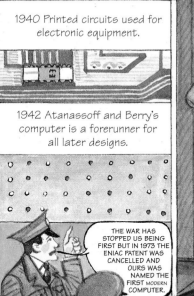
1940 Printed circuits used for electronic equipment.

1942 Atanassoff and Berry's computer is a forerunner for all later designs.

THE WAR HAS STOPPED US BEING FIRST BUT IN 1973 THE ENIAC PATENT WAS CANCELLED AND OURS WAS NAMED THE FIRST MODERN COMPUTER.

MAYBE I'LL PRESS THIS ONE ...

1948 De Mestral discovers the idea of velcro-fastening after a walk with his dog.

1946 Libby uses the carbon-14 method for dating archaeological objects.

I DON'T FEEL A DAY OVER 10,000 ...

1943 Koff develops the first kidney dialysis machine.

1947 Gabor outlines the idea of holography though it will need lasers (1960s) to make it work.

1948 Goldmark invents the long-playing record.

THE ENIAC COMPUTER COULD MAKE 5000 ADDITIONS AND 1000 MULTIPLICATIONS PER HOUR.

1947 The Dead Scrolls – Jewish documents from Christ's time – are found by two shepherd boys.

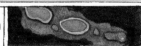
1942 Rober makes the first 'radio' maps of the Universe.

1947 The first supersonic aeroplane flight takes place in America.

1948 The term 'bug' (meaning a computer malfunction) is coined in Manchester when a moth supposedly gets into electronic circuitry.

1940 The Tacoma Narrow Bridge collapses because it is not aerodynamically stable.

1941-45 Millions of Jews are killed with gas in Nazi concentration camps.

1944 Avery, MacLeod and McCarthy say that DNA is the hereditary material for most life.

1940-45 British cities bombed – blitzed by the Luftwaffe. German cities are bombed in return.

1901 Enrico Fermi 1954

ATOM

In 1938 the Italian physicist, Enrico Fermi, went as a political refugee to the United States where he worked as an atomic researcher. With his fellow researcher, Leo Szilard, he succeeded in building an 'atomic pile' in a squash court at Chicago University. It was the first atomic reactor and used uranium to create the first nuclear chain reaction.

Fermi's first attempt at fission produced only half a Watt of energy, but it was an important step in the history of invention. It enabled scientists working on the Manhattan Project in New Mexico to successfully develop an atomic bomb.

The work of Fermi and his group and their 1942 discovery also enabled other physicists to develop modern reactors capable of generating huge amounts of nuclear energy.

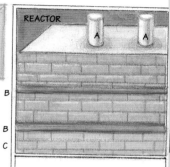

REACTOR

A. Fuel rods — cylinders of Uranium.

B. Cadmium rods to absorb neutrons and control fission.

C. Graphite, to act as a moderator.

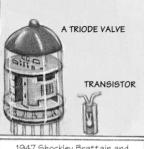

A TRIODE VALVE

TRANSISTOR

1947 Edwin Land invents the Polaroid camera.

1947 Shockley Brattain and Bardeen invent the transistor. Tiny transistors replace valves so that smaller computers can be made.

1943 The first SCUBA (self-contained underwater breathing apparatus) is developed when Gagnan adds a regulating valve to Cousteau's Aqua-Lung.

1947 Buckminster Fuller patents the geodesic dome.

FERMI WAS ONE OF THE MOST IMPORTANT MEN OF THE NUCLEAR AGE.

1943 Penicillin is first used in the treatment of chronic diseases.

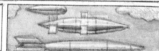

1944 Germany launches the V1, a flying bomb, and the V2 the first long-range ballistic missile.

1945 The United Nations is founded and based in New York.

1941 Japanese planes attack a US naval base at Pearl Harbour, Hawaii.

1942–44 The Diary of Anne Frank is written.

1940 Prehistoric wall paintings are found in France.

1947 Thor Heyerdahl's expedition from Peru to Polynesia takes place.

1945 The US explodes atomic bombs over Nagasaki and Hiroshima, ending World War II.

1910 CHRISTOPHER COCKERELL 1999

HIGH FREQUENCY SOUND WAVES

1955 Donald uses ultrasound to study unborn babies.

1955 Chapin, Fuller and Person develop a photovoltaic (solar) cell to make energy from sunlight.

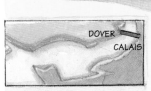

1955 Kapany invents optical fibres.

Christopher Cockerell was a radio engineer turned boat-builder whose investigations into the problems of water-drag led to his inventing the hovercraft in 1955. It was based on a wonderfully simple idea and could fly over the surface of land and water on just a few inches of cushioned air. Cockerell developed his first simple model from an assortment of tins of different sizes, some kitchen scales and a vacuum cleaner motor. When air was pumped into the ring between the tins it became compressed, and the thrust set up a hover.

His SR-NI hovercraft, which at 65 knots could travel twice the speed of a normal ferry boat, crossed the English Channel exactly 50 years after Blériot's first aeroplane flight over the Channel.

DOVER
CALAIS

THE HOVERCRAFT TEST FLIGHT TAKES PLACE 50 YEARS AFTER BLÉRIOT'S FAMOUS FLIGHT ACROSS THE CHANNEL.

1959 Kilby devises the first integrated circuit (a single electronic component).

1957 Sputnik 1, the first artificial satellite, is launched by the USSR.

1971 floppy disc developed by an IBM team led by Alan Shugart.

LOGICAL REASONING + FORMAL CALCULUS =

1956 Newell, Shaw and Simon invent Artificial Intelligence programming languages.

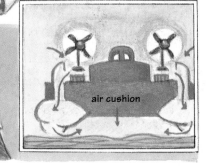

air cushion

THE DRAMATIC APPEARANCE OF THE HOVERCRAFT CAUSED A SENSATION.

1958 An American satellite successfully orbits the Earth.

1957 Gould first thinks up the possibility of lasers, but fails to patent his idea.

1958 The space station, NASA, is set up in America.

1956 Jorn Utzon designs the Sydney Opera House.

1956 Martin Luther King campaigns for desegregation of the races in America.

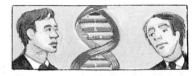

1953 Watson and Crick make a double helix model for deoxyribonucleic.

I'M ALL SHOOK UP!

1956 The Rock and Roll dance and music era begins with singers like Elvis Presley.

GASP!!

1955 3D Films are introduced.

1927 Theodore Maiman

The laser – Light Amplification by the Stimulated Emission of Radiation – was invented by the American physicist Theodore Maiman in May 1960.

At first no-one could think of many ways to use the new invention but, by 1964, it was being used to carry out eye surgery.

Now lasers are used in hundreds of ways: in industry, for cutting and welding; in engineering, for measuring and surveying; in medicine, for eye surgery and many other operations; in military and space technology; in telecommunications, for carrying signals. Lasers are used to produce compact discs and holograms, and for computing and printing.

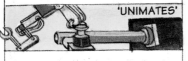
1965 Engelbart makes the first mouse to help operators interact naturally with their computers.

'UNIMATES'
1962 The first industrial robot is introduced.

HIGH FIDELITY
1967 Dolby invents his system to reduce background sound on audio equipment.

ESSA-1
1960s NASA launches telecommunication (Telstar 1962) and weather (ESSA-1 1966) satellites.

A NITINOL ELEPHANT NEVER FORGETS.
1960 Bueler invents Nitinol – a nickel-titanium alloy – which changes shape with temperature, but 'remembers' its original moulded shape.

1968 NASA recognition for Francis and Gertrude Rogallo's 'Flexible Kite' design (used in space capsule landings).

light shield

mirror

semi-silvered mirror

glass jacket to cool laser

power

ruby crystal rod

released heat and red laser light energy

In the crystal rod, light energy excites the atoms, and they too release energy.

incoherent light

torch

coherent light

laser

1964 The first lasers were used in delicate surgery, like the repairing of a detached retina in the eye.

AT FIRST NO-ONE COULD FIND A PRACTICAL USE FOR MAIMAN'S LASER.

1968 Lake Erie is pronounced 'dead'.

1962 Rachel Carson's 'Silent Spring' attacks pesticide pollution.

1969 Solar Furnace at Odeillo, France.

ENVIRONMENTAL WORRIES BEGIN TO SURFACE • ECOLOGICAL AWARENESS • SUPPORT FOR RENEWABLE ENERGY

I KNOW PEOPLE THAT DENSE
1963 Theory of 'Black Holes' – stars so dense that no light can escape the gravity.

VOSTOK I
1961 Gagarin of the USSR is the first man in space.

1969 An American, Neil Armstrong, is the first man to walk on the moon.

1963 The US president John Kennedy is shot in Dallas, Texas.

1960s Cold war tension between USA and USSR.

The SEVENTIES

1971 At Intel, Silicon Valley, Marcian Hoff invents the Microchip, the key development which makes micro-computers possible.

1970 Floppy disc continues to be developed to store computer data.

No one inventor dominated the 1970s but many exciting developments and much innovation took place.

In 1971 at Intel, Silicon Valley, the American, Marcian Hoff, invented the Microchip. In 1972, the first pocket calculator, invented by Kilby, Merryman, and Van Tassel of Texas Instruments, became available. The first personal computer, Apple II, appeared in 1977. And in 1979 Akio Morita of Sony invented the Personal Stereo or Walkman.

Optical fibres now allowed one single fibre to carry 20,000 telephone calls. Spy, information and communications satellites beamed information back to earth. Space probes, like Pioneer and Viking, gathered vast amounts of information about the planets, and Skylab and Salyut space laboratories were launched and sent back information about our own planet, earth.

1979 The 'Walkman', a portable miniaturized cassette unit with headphones, is devised by Akio Morita.

1979 Philips and Sony jointly develop the compact disc.

1971 The first magnetic levitation train is developed in Japan.

1970s Using microprocessor (microchip) technology MIT (with the Altair) and Apple bring out personal computers.

1973 Liquid crystals are used for watch and pocket calculator displays.

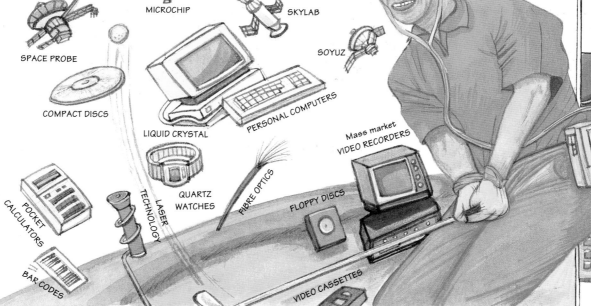
SPACE PROBE · MICROCHIP · SKYLAB · SOYUZ · SATELLITES · COMPACT DISCS · LIQUID CRYSTAL · PERSONAL COMPUTERS · POCKET CALCULATORS · LASER TECHNOLOGY · QUARTZ WATCHES · FIBRE OPTICS · Mass market VIDEO RECORDERS · FLOPPY DISCS · BAR CODES · VIDEO CASSETTES

1970s The USSR and USA set up space stations, space probes, and specialized satellites.

They send back detailed data from space by digital transmission.

CABLE · QUARTZ GLASS

1977 Fibre optic cables are first used for telephone systems.

1972 Kilby, Merryman and van Tassel develop the pocket calculator.

AKIO MORITA WANTED TO LISTEN TO MUSIC AND PLAY GOLF AT THE SAME TIME.

1974 Chicago's Sears Tower, the world's tallest building.

1974 Lucy, a 3 million year old 'hominid' is discovered in Africa.

1976 In Seveso, Italy, a pesticide factory releases poisonous dioxins.

1978 The first 'test-tube' baby is born.

ENVIRONMENTAL ACCIDENTS IN THE 1970s

1970s Famine in Africa.

1979 Partial meltdown at Three Mile Island reactor in America.

1978 The AIDS virus is first recognised.

1974 US President Nixon resigns over the Watergate scandal.

1980s AND 1990s

> THE CRAY I CAN MAKE 150 MILLION CALCULATIONS PER SECOND.

In these decades, space shuttles and magnetic levitation (MAGLEV) trains – the cutting edge of transport technology – were there to carry us into the next century. But it was computing that came of age.

Research teams at IBM, and Apple's new desktop Macintosh machine made computing very user-friendly. Cray's super computers and industrial robots, like Japan's WAHL-11, were perfected from earlier models. In the 1980s Virtual Reality began its interactive computer-generated life. Some information technologists even began to consider carrying electronic data in light particles (optical computers) or molecules (biological computers).

1990 Cobe (Cosmic Background Explorer) is launched in the US on a Delta rocket to research the Big Bang, 15 billion years ago.

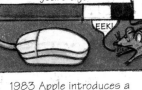

1983 Apple introduces a mouse and pull-down menu to its personal computers.

The first CRAY, 1976. 1980s Supercomputers ('number-crunchers') develop By 1988 the CRAY Y-MP is able to make 2 billion calculations per second.

CANON

1985 A laser colour photocopier is invented using laser and computer technology.

Pressing the mouse from a certain location sends a particular command to the computer.

1991 recordable CD marketed by Sony and Taiyo Yuden. It had been worked on since 1989.

1983 The camcorder prototype is devised by Sanyo and Philips.

1988 Zimmerman and Harvill develop a 'data glove' fitted with optic strands.

1980s IBM and Apple develop their personal computers (PCs), IBM (1981-87) introduce DOS (disc operating system), a hard disc memory device, and a new memory chip to increase speed and memory. Apple's Lisa technology make PCs powerful, but still affordable.

1980 Popular tiny aircraft, microlights, reach into the market.

1988 The joint European Torus machine reaches a temperature of 100 million K, 10 times hotter than the Sun, in an attempt to show the feasibility of controlled nuclear fusion.

1980s Lasers are used for holography, medicine (ariteries and tumours and 'smart' weapons.

1988 Muller and Bednorz invent a superconducting ceramic material, which works at warmer temperatures. Practical uses for super conductors include Raj and Moons frictionless bearings.

1990 BILL GATES INTRODUCED THE EASY-TO-USE WINDOWS 3.0 SOFTWARE FOR IBM PCS.

1986 The voyager aircraft flies around the world without refuelling.

FLIGHT

> GLASNOST and PERESTROIKA

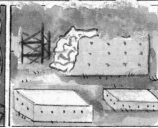

1980s Tropical rainforests are rapidly destroyed.

1980 Smallpox is eradicated.

THE ENVIRONMENT

1997 Dolly the Sheep is cloned by Scientists in Rosslyn, Scotland.

1986 The Challenger space shuttle explodes just after take off, and its crew are killed.

1987 Presidents Gorbachev and Reagan meet to discuss arms reductions.

1986 Chernobyl: a nuclear accident sends radioactive fallout over Europe.

1980 Solutions to environmental problems are actively sought.

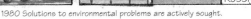

Organic farming   Lead-free petrol   Catalytic converter

THE NEW MILLENNIUM

The next generation may live for 150 years, if research into ageing and replacement body-parts are successful. Scientists could in the future develop a total DNA map, the human genome, enabling us to 'read' illness-causing genes, and be treated with transgenic technology.

The first permanent international orbiting space station is in progress. Space explorers aboard may be able to terraform neighbouring planets, then fly back to Earth in a Hotol, a shuttle which acts as both a plane and a rocket.

But perhaps the greatest challenge of the 21st century lies in solving our environmental problems. We must turn to the next generation of inventors to find ways of helping us to protect our planet.

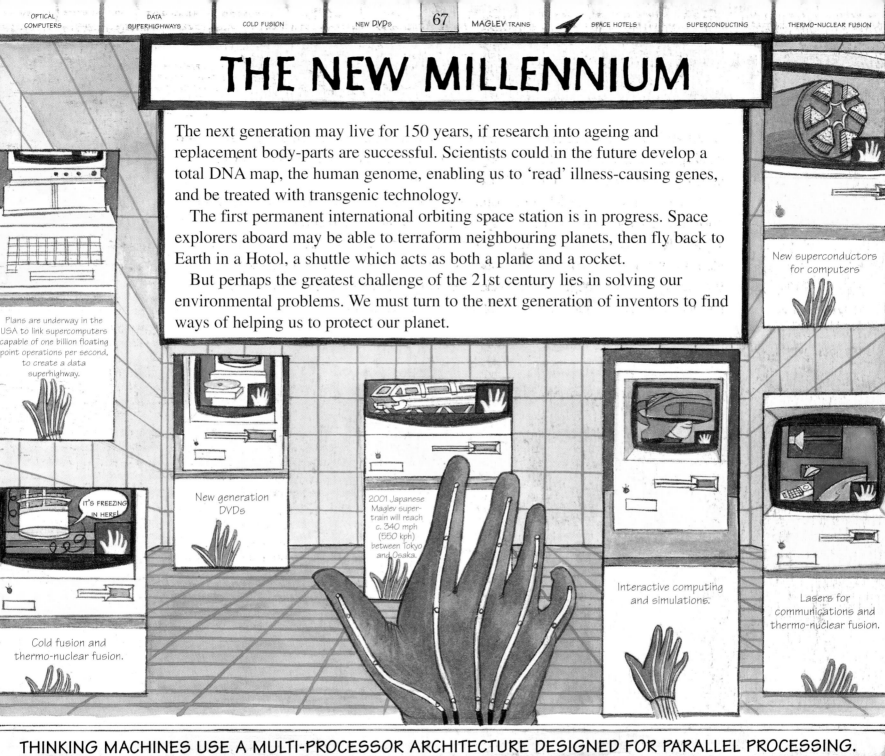

THINKING MACHINES USE A MULTI-PROCESSOR ARCHITECTURE DESIGNED FOR PARALLEL PROCESSING.

10 years after the fall of the Berlin Wall can Europe unite under a single European currency (ECU)?

The Shimizu Corporation has already designed a space hotel to be opened in the year 2020.

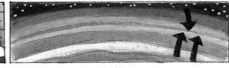

Will we see the end of racism and discrimination?

CFCs and ozone depletion.

How will we deal with climatic changes and the longterm effects of pollution?

GLOSSARY

A

Aerodynamics The study of forces acting on bodies moving through gases or the air.

Aerosol Particles dispersed in a gas (i.e. a mist), or a pressurized container with a spray nozzle, which shoots out an 'aerosol'.

Amperemeter/Ammeter An instrument that measures an electric current.

Anaesthetic A drug that causes the loss of sensation to touch, pain and heat.

Animalcule A microscopic animal.

Antiseptic A chemical or other agent which destroys or prevents the growth of bacteria.

Archimedes' screw A screw-like device for raising water. One end of the hollow tube is placed in water and when the screw is turned, the water rises to a higher level.

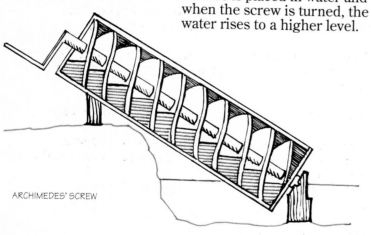

ARCHIMEDES' SCREW

Artificial intelligence A branch of computer science, and also the idea that computers might be programmed to learn and reason, adapt, and self-correct, as with human intelligence.

Asteroid One of many thousands of tiny, rocky, planetary bodies to be found going round the Sun, between the orbits of Mars and Jupiter.

Astrolabe An instrument used by early navigators to measure the altitude of the Sun and stars. It can tell the time, find latitude, and calculate the future positions of the Sun and the brightest stars.

ASTROLABE

Astronomy The science of the 'heavens' (i.e. of the planets other than the Earth), and of the Universe.

Atom The smallest particle of an element that is able to take part in a chemical reaction.

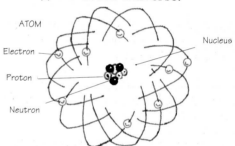

ATOM

Electron

Proton

Neutron

Nucleus

Atomic pile The name of the original nuclear reactor. (The pile of graphite blocks was used to moderate a nuclear chain reaction.)

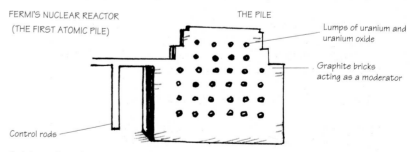

FERMI'S NUCLEAR REACTOR
(THE FIRST ATOMIC PILE)

THE PILE

Lumps of uranium and uranium oxide

Graphite bricks acting as a moderator

Control rods

Cadmium rods to absorb neutrons and control atomic fission

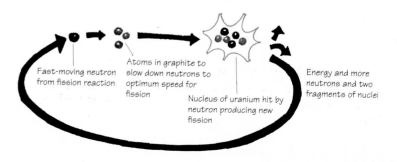

Fast-moving neutron from fission reaction

Atoms in graphite to slow down neutrons to optimum speed for fission

Nucleus of uranium hit by neutron producing new fission

Energy and more neutrons and two fragments of nuclei

Axis powers   The alliance of Nazi Germany, Fascist Italy, and Japan from 1936 to its defeat by the 'Allies' at the end of World War II.

B

Backstaff   A navigational instrument used to measure the Sun's altitude: so called because users have their back to the Sun, and look at a point of light shining onto a scale, instead of being dazzled by looking directly at the Sun.

Bacteria   A large group of variously-shaped microscopic organisms. They can multiply rapidly and cause disease in plants and animals.

BACTERIA

Ballistics   The study of the changing path taken by an object, a missile for example, as it falls freely under the influence of gravity.

Barometer   An instrument to measure the pressure or weight of the atmosphere. It is useful for weather forecasting.

Bathysphere   A deep-sea steel diving sphere, which is lowered into position by cable.

Battery   The source of an electric current. The battery, made up of a group of cells, generates the electric current.

Biological computer   A brain is a natural 'biological computer', using living cells or 'slimeware', instead of electronic 'hardware', to process information. Artificial biological computers cannot yet be made.

Biology   The study of living organisms.

Bolsheviks   Members of Russia's Revolutionary Party, led by Lenin, which seized power in 1917.

C

Caesarian birth/section   The delivery of a baby by cutting through the walls of the mother's abdomen and womb. Sometimes it is safer for a baby to be born like this.

Calculus   A branch of mathematics which deals with the calculation of constantly varying quantities.

Calorimeter   An apparatus used for measuring heat.

Calotype process   Fox Talbot's method for making a photographic image.

Camera obscura   A large box, or darkened chamber, with a double convex lens at one end. Images of surrounding objects can be focused on a screen at the other end.

Camphor   A whitish aromatic substance distilled originally from camphor trees and used for making celluloid, a type of plastic.

Carbon dating   A method of dating organic material such as wood, bone, leather, ivory, or cloth, by measuring the proportion of radioactive to non-radioactive carbon present.

Cartographer   A person who draws and prepares maps.

Cast iron   A hard, brittle iron produced by smelting ores. It contains impurities, especially carbon.

Catalytic converter   A device which reduces the amount of pollutants emitted in a car's exhaust.

Cellulose   The carbohydrate substance making up plant cell walls, and used in the manufacture of paper, fabrics, paints and plastics.

Centrifugal   The tendency to fly away from the centre.

Chain reaction   A chemical or an atomic process. Products of a chain reaction continue and accelerate the process by reacting with the original chemical or atomic substances.

Chip   A popular name for an integrated circuit, made on a chip, or flat, wafer-thin section, of silicon.

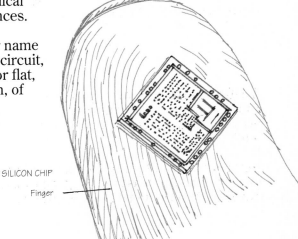

SILICON CHIP

Finger

Cinematograph An instrument for making 'motion' pictures. Pictures of instant (still) photographs of moving objects are projected onto a screen, giving the illusion of motion.

Computer An electronic machine that makes calculations by storing data, and using a program to work on the data.

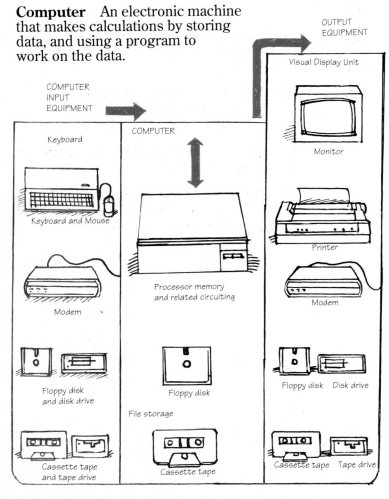

COMPUTER INPUT EQUIPMENT

Keyboard

Keyboard and Mouse

Modem

Floppy disk and disk drive

Cassette tape and tape drive

COMPUTER

Processor memory and related circuiting

Floppy disk

File storage

Cassette tape

OUTPUT EQUIPMENT

Visual Display Unit

Monitor

Printer

Modem

Floppy disk   Disk drive

Cassette tape   Tape drive

Condenser (engineering) A chamber where exhaust steam from a steam engine or turbine is cooled and condensed to make a partial vacuum.

Conductor A material that allows the passage of an electric current.

Connecting rod In an engine or a pump, the rod connecting the piston and the crank.

Convex Curving outwards, like the outside of a circle.

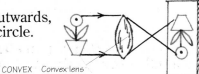

CONVEX   Convex lens

Copernicus/Copernican system The theory of planetary motion which says that the Sun is at the centre of the Solar System, and the planets (including the earth) revolve around it.

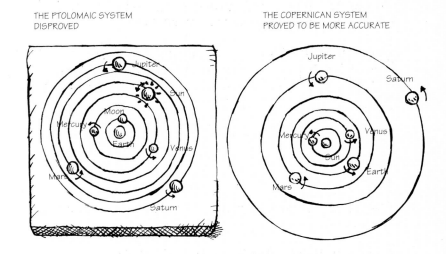

THE PTOLOMAIC SYSTEM DISPROVED

THE COPERNICAN SYSTEM PROVED TO BE MORE ACCURATE

Crank An L-shaped arm attached to a shaft. It transfers up-and-down motion into the circular motion of the shaft.

Crankshaft The main shaft on an engine or other machine, on which one or more cranks are carried, and are attached to connecting rods.

D

Dialysis The process of purifying the blood of impurities in an artificial kidney.

Digital computer A computer that uses coded on-off electrical signals representing digits (numbers) to solve numerical problems.

Diode An electronic device that allows current to flow in one direction only.

DNA Deoxyribose nucleic acid; a double-stranded form of genetic material found in the chromosomes. It stores genetic information and is responsible for transmitting hereditary characteristics from parents to their children.

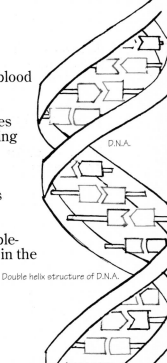

D.N.A.

Double helix structure of D.N.A.

Dirigible   A navigable balloon or airship.

Dynamics   A branch of physics dealing with matter in motion and how it is affected by a force or forces.

Dynamite   A powerful nitro-glycerine explosive packed into an absorbent substance to make it safer.

Dynamo   A machine that converts mechanical energy into electrical energy.

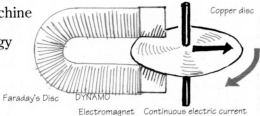

Faraday's Disc   DYNAMO
Copper disc
Electromagnet   Continuous electric current

E

Electricity   A form of energy that is found in a proton or an electron.

Electro magnet   A soft iron core within a current-carrying coil of wire. When an electric current passes through the wire the iron becomes magnetized.

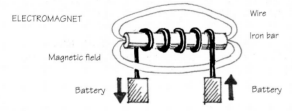

ELECTROMAGNET
Wire
Iron bar
Magnetic field
Battery   Battery

Elasticity   The ability of a body to return to its normal size or shape after being stretched, contracted or distorted.

Embryology   The study of embryos – the early formation and development of immature organisms.

Electric motor   A device that converts electrical energy into mechanical movement (rotation) in a mechanism.

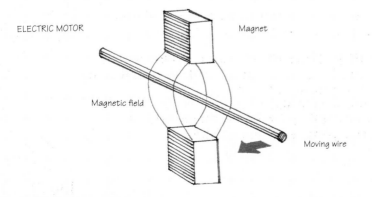

ELECTRIC MOTOR
Magnet
Magnetic field
Moving wire

Electron   A particle with a negative electrical charge, forming part of an atom.

Electronic devices   such as television tubes, electron microscopes, and silicon chips that rely on the movement of electrons.

Engine   A machine in which energy (the heat or chemical energy of fuel) is converted into mechanical work.

Engineer   *Civil*   A person skilled in making and maintaining works of public utility like bridges, roads, canals etc.

Mechanical   A person skilled in making and maintaining machines.

Electrical   A person skilled in the production and transmission of electric energy, and the manufacture of electrical appliances.

CIVIL ENGINEER
Brunel

MECHANICAL ENGINEER
Benz

Visionary ideas, plans, calculations,
Good hands for dexterity

ELECTRICAL ENGINEER
Edison

Visionary ideas
Large head for brains, problem-solving etc.

Brains   Capacious pockets for earnings from many inventions

Euclid   A mathematician from Alexandria (3rd century BC), the author of a *treatise* on geometry.

F

Fertilization   The fusion of a male reproductive cell with a female one.

Fermentation (chemistry)   The slow decomposition of organic substances caused, for example, by micro-organisms or enzymes of plant or animal origin, and usually giving off heat and gas.

Floppy disk   A lightweight flexible magnetic disk which behaves as if rigid when rotated rapidly. Used to hold information in a personal computer.

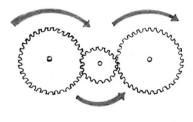

FLOPPY DISK

G

Galvanometer   A device for detecting and measuring the strength of an electric current.

Gear   A group of moving parts (such as toothed wheels or levers) which transmits motion.

GEARS

Geiger counter   An instrument which detects and measures ionizing radiation, such as that emitted by radioactive materials.

Graphite   A black soft form of natural crystalline carbon, used in pencils.

H

Heredity   The relationship between successive generations, and how children inherit the nature and characteristics of their parents or ancestors.

Holography   A photographic technique using lasers, which gives a three-dimensional picture of an object.

Hydraulics   The science dealing with the flow of fluids, e.g. when water or oil is conveyed through pipes under pressure and used to operate machines like cranes, brakes, etc.

Hydrofoil   A fast light craft, like a motorboat, fitted with fin-like structures (foils) on struts under the hull. These lift the hull out of the water at speed.

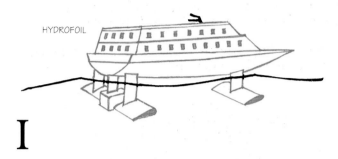

HYDROFOIL

I

Iconoscope   One of the first electronic TV camera tubes, developed by scientists at RCA (the Radio Corporation of America).

Ignition   The firing of an explosive mixture of gases, vapours, or other substances, usually by means of an electric spark (especially in the cylinder of an internal combustion engine).

Internal combustion engine   An engine in which the combustion and expansion of a fuel (the mixture of petrol, or oil, or gas, and air) takes place inside the cylinders and produces motive power.

INTERNAL COMBUSTION ENGINE

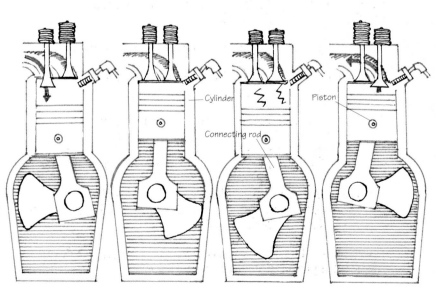

L

Laser (Light Amplification by Stimulated Emission of Radiation). A device which produces a narrow, intense beam of light of a single colour, in which all the light waves are in phase.

Lathe A machine for producing cylindrical work by turning materials such as wood, metal, and ivory.

Lever A very simple machine in which a rigid beam is pivoted at a point called a fulcrum.

LEVER

Lithography The art of printing from a stone or metal surface, relying on the mutual repulsion of water and greasy ink.

M

Malleable iron The type of iron which can be altered by hammering, beating, rolling etc. without returning to its original form.

Manometer An instrument used to measure the pressure of a gas or liquid.

Mass (physics) The quantity of matter in a body.

Microbe A micro-organism, especially one of the bacteria causing disease or fermentation.

Microchip/Microprocessor A computer's central processing unit (CPU) found in one or more integrated-circuit chips. It may be the main element of a microcomputer or a portion of an automatic control system.

Microcomputer A small, usually inexpensive, computer, using a microprocessor which enables the size to be greatly reduced.

Molecule The smallest portion of a substance which has all the properties of the substance.

N

Nucleus (physics) The core of an atom which takes up most of its mass. The nucleus is composed of protons (positively charged) and neutrons (no charge) and is surrounded by orbiting electrons (negatively charged).

NUCLEUS

O

Offset printing The process by which the ink from a printing plate is received onto a rubber-coated cylinder, and from which it is then transferred onto paper or another material.

Optical fibre This is a thin strand of pure glass which can transmit light by total internal reflection.

OPTICAL FIBRES

Thin threads of extremely pure glass

A single fibre

Plastic sheath
Cladding
Glass core

Oxides Compounds of oxygen with another element, often formed at high temperatures.

P

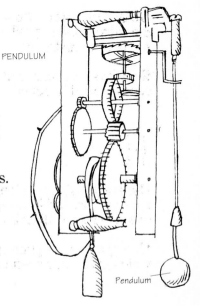

PENDULUM

Parabola A form of curve.

Pendulum A small, heavy body suspended from a fixed point, and able to swing freely. In clocks, a pendulum is used to regulate the movement of the clock's works.

Physicist A person who studies the properties and nature of matter, forms of energy, and the mutual interaction of energy and matter.

Pendulum

Piston   A short metal cylinder within a cylindrical vessel, which moves to and fro by fluid pressure (e.g. in an engine), or which compresses and displaces a fluid (as in a pump).

Pneumatics   The science of the mechanical properties of air and other gases.

Polarization (e.g. of light) To restrict the vibrations of transverse waves to one plane.

Probability   The likelihood of an event occurring, measured mathematically.

Proton   A fundamental atomic particle forming part (or, for hydrogen, the whole) of the nucleus. It has a positive charge, equal and opposite to the negative charge of the electron.

Pulley   A simple mechanism where a grooved wheel, carrying a belt or cord is mounted in a block and is used, for example, for lifting weights.

R

Radioactivity   The property of atoms of some elements (for example, uranium, radium, thorium) to spontaneously disintegrate and emit ionizing radiation (in the form of alpha particles, beta particles, and gamma rays).

Radio waves   Electromagnetic waves by which messages are transmitted and received.

Receiver   Usually the part of radio, television, telegraph or telephone needed to convert electrical or other signals into a message.

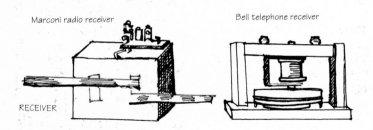

RADIOACTIVITY

α Alpha particle — Parent nucleus — γ Gamma ray — Daughter nucleus — β Beta particle

Marconi radio receiver / Bell telephone receiver / RECEIVER

S

Steam engine   An external combustion engine where steam is the working fluid.

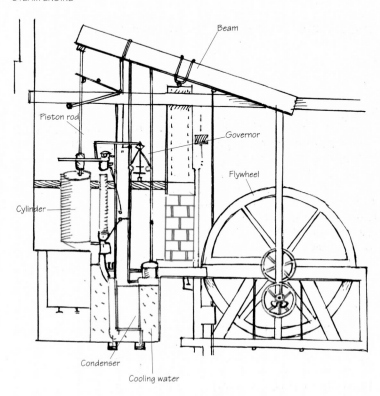

STEAM ENGINE — Beam, Piston rod, Governor, Flywheel, Cylinder, Condenser, Cooling water

Sterilization (of an object)   To free from contamination by removing unwanted micro-organisms, using heat, radiation, antiseptic chemicals or filtration.

Stratosphere   The atmosphere above the troposphere, where the temperature does not decrease with height.

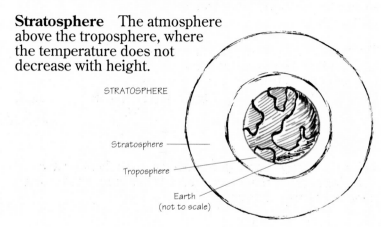

STRATOSPHERE — Stratosphere, Troposphere, Earth (not to scale)

Supercomputer   A powerful, high performance mainframe computer used for solving scientific numerical problems.

Superconductivity   The property of some substances (some pure metals or metallic alloys) of having no resistance to the flow of an electric current at very low temperatures.

Supersonic   Faster than the speed of sound.

T

Telegraphy   The old name for communicating certain material (written, pictorial or printed matter) at a distance. Wireless telegraphy is the transmission of signals through space by the means of electromagnetic waves.

Television   The electronic transmission, reception and reproduction of moving-pictures.

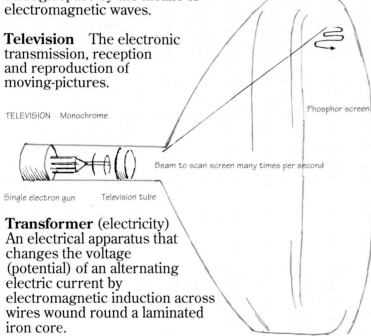

TELEVISION   Monochrome

Phosphor screen

Beam to scan screen many times per second

Single electron gun   Television tube

Transformer (electricity) An electrical apparatus that changes the voltage (potential) of an alternating electric current by electromagnetic induction across wires wound round a laminated iron core.

Transmitter   Usually the part of radio, television, telegraph or telephone needed to produce electrical or other signals to transmit a message.

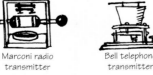

TRANSMITTER

Marconi radio transmitter

Bell telephone transmitter

Triode   A vacuum tube or electronic amplifying valve containing three main electrodes (a cathode, anode, and control electrode, or grid).

Troposphere   The lower part of the atmosphere, from the Earth's surface up to the stratosphere, in which the temperature decreases regularly with height.

Turbine   A motor in which rotary motion is produced by a fluid (like water, steam or gas) which directly turns blades, and the cylinder attached to them, to produce power for driving ships, aircraft, or generators of electricity, for example.

U

Ultrasound   The high-pitched sound of a frequency above 20KHz used by animals like bats and dolphins, and by humans, for medical purposes like scanning tissues.

V

Vacuum   A space entirely empty of matter. On Earth, usually only a partial vacuum is possible. These 'vacuums' are used in cleaners and braking systems etc.

Virtual Reality   Computer-based systems which allow users to explore simulated or imaginary environments.

Vulcanized rubber   The treatment of rubber with compounds such as sulphur that make it harder and more durable.

W

WINDLASS

Windlass   A simple mechanical contrivance for hauling and hoisting.

X

X-rays   Short wavelength electromagnetic waves, produced when high-speed electrons strike a solid target.

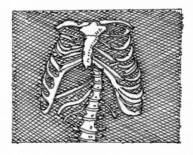

INDEX

MORE SCIENCE AND INFORMATION TITLES IN PAPERBACK FROM FRANCES LINCOLN

UNTIL I MET DUDLEY
Roger McGough
Illustrated by Chris Riddell

Have you ever wondered how a toaster works? Or how a fridge keeps cool?
Well, now you can discover all the answers with the help of Dudley, the techno-wizard dog
in this fun-filled investigation into how everyday things really work.

Suitable for National Curriculum English – Reading, Key Stage 2
Scottish Guidelines English Language – Reading, Levels B and C;
Environmental Studies, Levels B and C

ISBN 0-7112-1129-9 £5.99

THE DROP IN MY DRINK
Meredith Hooper
Illustrated by Chris Coady

This exciting follow-up to *The Pebble in my Pocket* follows a drop of water from
the Earth's beginnings, showing how and when the Earth got its water,
the relationship between water and living things, and the water cycle.

Suitable for National Curriculum English – Reading, Key Stages 2 and 3;
Geography, Key Stage 3
Scottish Guidelines English Language – Reading, Level D;
Environmental Studies, Levels C and D

ISBN 0-7112-1182-5 £5.99

HOW GREEN ARE YOU?
Dr. David Bellamy
Illustrated by Penny Dann

The friendly Whale leads us on a tour of our every-day habitat, explaining how
we can protect the environment at every step.

Suitable for National Curriculum Science, Key Stages 1 and 2;
Geography, Key Stages 1 and 2
Scottish Guidelines Environmental Studies, Levels B and C

ISBN 0-7112-0679-1 £5.99

Frances Lincoln titles are available from all good bookshops
Prices are correct at time of publication, but may be subject to change